SCIENCE, TECHNOLOGY AND INNOVATION POLICIES

DENMARK

ORGANISATION FOR ECONOMIC CO-OPERATION AND DEVELOPMENT

ORGANISATION FOR ECONOMIC CO-OPERATION AND DEVELOPMENT

Pursuant to Article 1 of the Convention signed in Paris on 14th December 1960, and which came into force on 30th September 1961, the Organisation for Economic Co-operation and Development (OECD) shall promote policies designed:

— to achieve the highest sustainable economic growth and employment and a rising standard of living in Member countries, while maintaining financial stability, and thus to contribute to the development of the world economy;

— to contribute to sound economic expansion in Member as well as non-member countries in the process of economic development; and

— to contribute to the expansion of world trade on a multilateral, non-discriminatory basis in accordance with international obligations.

The original Member countries of the OECD are Austria, Belgium, Canada, Denmark, France, Germany, Greece, Iceland, Ireland, Italy, Luxembourg, the Netherlands, Norway, Portugal, Spain, Sweden, Switzerland, Turkey, the United Kingdom and the United States. The following countries became Members subsequently through accession at the dates indicated hereafter: Japan (28th April 1964), Finland (28th January 1969), Australia (7th June 1971), New Zealand (29th May 1973) and Mexico (18th May 1994). The Commission of the European Communities takes part in the work of the OECD (Article 13 of the OECD Convention).

Publié en français sous le titre :

POLITIQUES DE LA SCIENCE, DE LA TECHNIQUE ET DE L'INNOVATION

DANEMARK

© OECD 1995

Applications for permission to reproduce or translate all or part of this publication should be made to:
Head of Publications Service, OECD
2, rue André-Pascal, 75775 PARIS CEDEX 16, France

FOREWORD

This report is part of the OECD series of Science, Technology and Innovation Policy Reviews of individual Member countries.

These reviews have two purposes. First to enable the country concerned to appraise the institutions and mechanisms which influence various fields – scientific and industrial, but also economic, educational and social – and contribute to its technological development. Second, to help enrich the available knowledge of the content of relevant policies. OECD countries can thus derive lessons which will help them to perfect their own policies. Finally, through this improved appreciation of the resources deployed by OECD countries, these reviews help to strengthen international co-operation.

The reviews are undertaken at the request of governments, which contribute to their cost. Although a flexible approach is adopted in regard to the focus, the methodology and the presentation of these reviews, there is a common procedure for preparing and conducting them. The process of review consists of the following stages:

- The preparation of a "Background Report" on the relevant features and policies of the country under review.
- An information mission: a team of "Examiners" – experts of a high standing chosen in the OECD countries – visits the country under review and contacts decision-makers, senior officials, industrialists and academics. The Examiners also visit a certain number of laboratories, universities, enterprises, and public and private institutions. The aim of the second stage is to supplement the information provided by the Background Report and to enable the Examiners to formulate the main problems raised by the implementation of the policies under review: these are presented in the "Examiners' Report".
- The presentation of the two reports to the OECD Committee for Scientific and Technological Policy, which then holds a Review Meeting at which representatives of the country under review answer questions put by the Examiners and the delegates of Member countries.
- The publication, on the authority of the Secretary-General, of all documents relating to the review; the Background Report, the Examiners' Report and the Account of the Review Meeting.

The different stages of the reviews took place in 1994. The review meeting was held in Copenhagen on 31 October 1994.

The Examiners and the OECD Directorate for Science, Technology and Industry would like to express their gratitude to the Danish authorities, and notably the officials of the Ministry of Research and the Ministry of Business and Industry who requested and supervised this study, particularly Ms. Vibeke Hein Olsen, Delegate of Denmark to the OECD Science and Technology Policy Committee and Mr. Bjarne Lundager Jensen. They provided invaluable assistance in this study and prepared related reports, meetings and visits.

Mr. Jean-Eric Aubert of the OECD Secretariat ensured the co-ordination of the review with the assistance of Mr. Hans Mieras.

This report is published on the responsibility of the Secretary-General of the OECD.

TABLE OF CONTENTS

BACKGROUND REPORT

EXAMINERS' REPORT

LIST OF TABLES

LIST OF FIGURES

BACKGROUND REPORT

PREFACE

It is the Danish Government's firm intention to strengthen national research efforts. Its goal is to raise total investments in research and development to a level equal to that of the other northern European countries before the year 2000. The research effort should be strengthened on a broad front, but high priority should be given to industry-related research in order to improve the ability of Danish enterprises to compete in the new world market.

The Danish science, technology and innovation system must be efficient and well-organised if Danish research is to be strengthened. For this reason, the Government has asked the OECD to review its structure. The intention is, first and foremost, to focus on the Danish system's ability to make its research results benefit industry and society.

The OECD has agreed to take on this task and has defined a framework and time schedule for the review. As usual for such national reviews, a background report must be presented, which describes the science, technology and innovation system, and focuses on the most pertinent problems of the country being reviewed.

The Danish Ministry of Research and the Danish Agency for Development of Trade and Industry have entrusted the Monday Morning Strategic Forum with this task, and it has been completed according to the instructions of the OECD. The consultants, however, were asked to write a background report offering a fresh and independent view of the Danish system. Consequently, it must be emphasised that the statements and conclusions of the report do not necessarily reflect the views of the Ministry of Research or those of the Danish Agency for Development of Trade and Industry, but only those of the Monday Morning Strategic Forum.

It is hoped that this background report will serve as the point of departure for a constructive debate on the future organisation of the Danish science, technology and innovation system.

A. O. Andersen
Minister of Research
May 1994

INTRODUCTION

Over the last ten years, the Danish science, technology and innovation (STI) system has undergone far-reaching changes in order to better meet the needs of society and of industry. The required transformation is by no means complete, and the system is now facing the new challenges presented by the general internationalisation of society.

Through the 1980s, changes in the STI system focused on giving society in general, as well as industry, "value for money". Furthermore, they aimed to stimulate interaction and transfer of knowledge among the various parts of the STI system. The changes in the STI system led to the creation of a series of institutions and tools directed towards fulfilling these objectives, notably a noteworthy increase in programme funding. This generated discussions of the limits of the STI strategy.

Thus, at the end of the 1980s and the beginning of the 1990s, elements of a new STI strategy, which gave more independence to the STI institutions, were implemented. Today, the focal point of discussion is whether those institutions have the will and the ability to exploit their "new freedom" and adapt to society's demands.

At the same time, the STI system is confronted with new challenges stemming from the general internationalisation of society. On the one hand, this implies a demand for more specialised competencies in the STI system, and, on the other, a demand for greater international interaction and mobility, while maintaining certain "special assets" within the Danish STI system. The essential issue is how the STI system fulfils such roles in society as:

– contributing to general scientific advances both nationally and internationally;
– providing the basis for higher education;
– supporting innovation in the business enterprise sector;
– supplying both the public and the public sector with the knowledge base for improving the quality of life;
– communicating new insights and understanding to the individual citizen by stimu-lating public debate, providing expert assessment to social debates, etc.

This report, however, focuses on the system itself – how it is organised with respect to funding institutions, advisory councils, etc. In other words, it focuses on the structural conditions that make it possible for the STI system to fulfil its role in society.

The report is structured as follows:

- Chapter I places the STI system in the context of the general challenge of internationalisation, before examining the Danish situation in the light of the main economic and political changes since the mid-1980s.
- Chapter II presents the key figures relating to the overall S&T effort in terms of R&D expenditures at national level, in the public sector and the business sector. Data on innovation-related expenditures are also provided with elements of comparison with other Nordic countries.
- Chapter III gives an overview of the ministerial and top-level advisory structure for STI, with special attention to the question of the role of the Ministry of Research and to the relationship between the national Research Councils and the Danish Council for Research Policy.
- Chapter IV focuses on the strategic programmes implemented since the mid-1980s; following a chronological presentation, their value for making STI activities more relevant to society, for stimulating interaction between institutions and sectors, and for simplifying administration, are brought out.
- Chapter V deals with public sector STI (at institutions of higher education and at government research institutes, etc.), with special attention to new structural initiatives, such as the Danish National Research Foundation, the Research Academy, the University Act, and PhD reform.
- Chapter VI addresses structural conditions and policies for STI activities in the business enterprise sector, with special attention to the technological service institutes and their current problems, to the funding of business enterprise STI activities, and to the issue of technology diffusion.
- Chapter VII turns to technology assessment and ethics and their institutionalisation in the Danish STI system, with an emphasis on barriers to further integration of technology assessment and ethics into actual activities and decisions in the STI system.
- Chapter VIII looks at the internationalisation of the STI system *via* a variety of international and regional, including specifically European, R&D programmes.

Organisation of the work

The present report has been drafted by the Monday Morning Strategic Forum.

It is based on extensive desk-research, 60 national and 40 international interviews with decision-makers at all levels on the STI system. A roundtable discussion on the preliminary conclusions from the interviews performed has been held with 40 participants in April 1994.

The work has been headed by Dr. Kim Møller, Research Director, Monday Morning Strategic Forum, assisted by Ms. Pia Mulvad Christiansen, Analyst, Monday Morning Strategic Forum. Mr. Tage Dræbye, Managing Director, Dræbye Management and Consulting, and Mr. Lars Klüver, Project Manager, Secretariat of the Danish Board of Technology have contributed to the work as consultants.

A Steering Committee has supervised the work and a national panel of experts has added valuable comments to several drafts of the report.

The Steering Committee consisted of Mr. Hugo von Linstow, Research Adviser, the Ministry of Education, Ms. Vibeke Hein Olsen, Head of Division, the Ministry of Research, and Ms. Birte Ougaard, Special Adviser, the Danish Agency for Development of Trade and Industry.

The Expert Panel consisted of Mr. Jens Frøslev Christensen, Associate Professor, the Copenhagen Business School, Associate Professor Dr. Tarja Cronberg, the Technical University of Denmark, Dr. Jørgen Kjems, Research Director, Risø National Laboratory, Dr. Jens Rostrup Nielsen, Research Director, Haldor Topsøe Ltd., Dr. Henrik Tvarnø, Rector, the University of Odense.

Finally, the report has been edited by the OECD Secretariat.

I. THE DANISH ECONOMY: RECENT TRENDS

This chapter gives a brief introduction to the Danish economy and the present economic situation. It discusses the problems of unemployment and the structural problem of production and export. As a complement to the economic and political discussions, major social developments in Denmark are identified. Finally, the chapter deals with the challenges of internationalisation of the STI sytem.

The previous Conservative-Liberal governments were able to improve macroeconomic conditions by bringing inflation and interest rates down and turning the trade and balance of payment deficits into surpluses. On the negative side, it left its successors, the present Social Democrat Government, a huge unemployment problem and structural problems of production and trade.

1. The economic transformation

The challenges of internationalisation are met differently in different countries. Denmark faces the same challenges as other countries, as well as the specific problems presented by unemployment and the composition of production/exports.

During the 1980s, the main goal of the Conservative-Liberal Government was to stabilise macroeconomic conditions, and, during the late 1980s in particular, the Danish economy largely managed to adapt to the new international economic reality.

Government expenditures remained at a very high level, owing both to increased expenditures on health, education, and social benefits, on the one hand, and to very heavy interest payments on government overseas debt, on the other (Figure I.1). Accordingly, government revenues had to remain high. This was – and still is – achieved by heavy taxation of personal income. However, corporate taxes were reduced from 50 to 40 per cent.

The government's primary objective was to switch from an economy with high inflation to an economy with low inflation, mainly through contractive monetary policies. Production was further internationalised as the balance of trade and payment deficits became surpluses. The main elements in the economic transformation of the late 1980s were:

Figure I.1. **Public expenditure as a percentage of GDP**

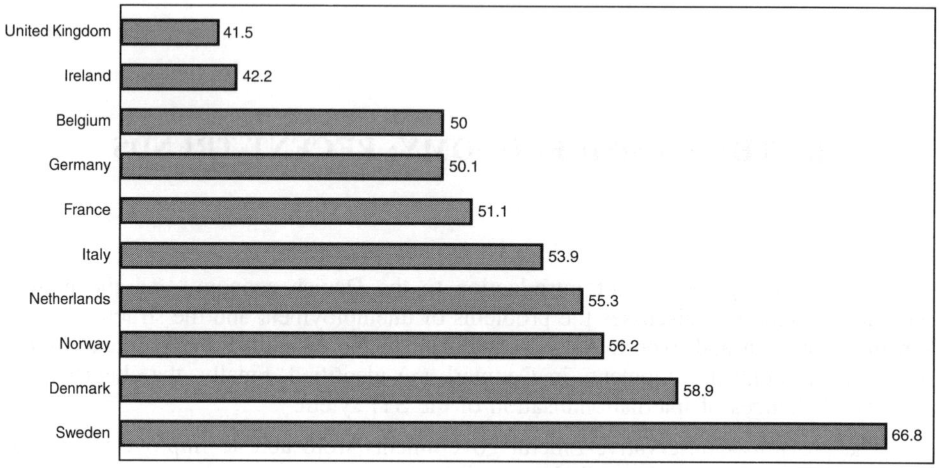

Country	Percentage
United Kingdom	41.5
Ireland	42.2
Belgium	50
Germany	50.1
France	51.1
Italy	53.9
Netherlands	55.3
Norway	56.2
Denmark	58.9
Sweden	66.8

Source: Ministry of Finance, Denmark, "Udgiftsanalyser 92".

- The so-called "potato diet" (1986) strongly limited domestic consumption, increased exports, and decreased imports. The depression of domestic consumption was in fact radical, and home market demand decreased faster than anticipated. At the same time, Danish companies lost important domestic market shares and unemployment rose to historic heights.
- The balance of payments deficit was turned to a surplus (Figure I.2). The net debt to banks and other lending institutions abroad now is 32 per cent of gross domestic product (GDP), but it was 41 per cent as late as 1988. On the other hand, government debt continued to increase owing to current government budget deficits, primarily caused by increased government expenditures related to unemployment. In 1991, government international debt amounted to DKr 351 billion, or 42 per cent of GDP.
- Converting the economy from high to low inflation started in fact in 1982, when the Danish currency was fixed within the European Monetary System (EMS), but the "potato diet" reinforced the trend from 1986 on. Lately, Denmark has had the lowest inflation rate in the world, with almost fixed prices. Costs associated with low inflation and fixed prices have increased post-tax real interest rates accordingly (see Figure I.3).
- High post-tax real interest rates have apparently further depressed domestic consumption, domestic economic growth, and thus industry investments. In fact,

Figure I.2. **Balance of payments and net debt**
Current prices

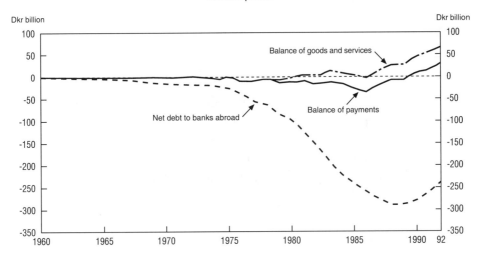

Source: Denmarks Statistik, ADAMs Databank.

Figure I.3. **Real post tax interest rate and inflation,1980-92**

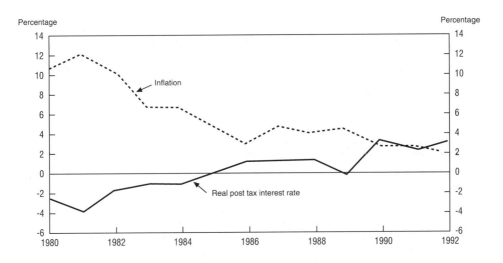

Source: Denmarks Statistik, ADAMs Databank.

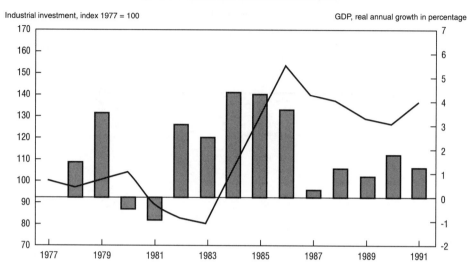

Figure I.4. **Industrial investment and GDP**

Industrial investment, index 1977 = 100

GDP, real annual growth in percentage

Source : Denmarks Statistik.

industry investments decreased during the late 1980s, lagging somewhat behind the development in domestic economic growth (Figure I.4).

The changes in the Danish economy have attracted considerable international interest and has even led to the term "the Danish miracle". At present, even considerable economic growth will not seriously affect the trade or balance of payment surplus.

2. The social challenge of unemployment

The cost of the Danish miracle is, first, a new world record, the economy with the lowest real economic growth since 1985, and second, ever increasing unemployment.

Since 1950, private employment has decreased by 63 000 persons in absolute terms. Growth in total employment from the 1960s through the 1980s has instead been due to public sector employment and the growing welfare state. For the last ten to 15 years, however, public sector employment has been stagnating, and the slow growth in private employment has been insufficient to absorb the increased number of entrants on the labour market. The official unemployment figures (Figure I.5) are now of the same order of magnitude as employment in the private business enterprise sector: 350 000 persons.

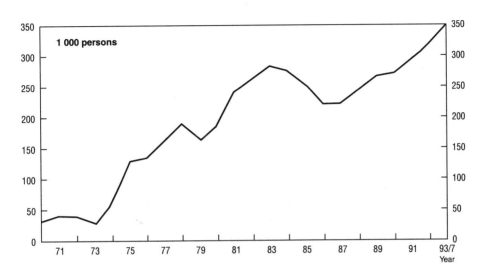

Figure I.5. **Unemployment 1970-93**

Source: Denmarks Statistik.

Thus, the government, led by Social Democrat Poul Nyrup Rasmussen, that took office in 1993 found a fairly strong economy in macroeconomic terms and a huge social challenge: how to avoid the polarisation of a society in which two-thirds of the population is employed and one-third is more or less permanently unemployed.

Since the new government came into power, this social challenge has attracted much political attention. New high-technology industries and jobs help solve the problem only to some extent, since the present unemployed workforce is unlikely to possess the requisite qualifications. Neither is growth in traditional industries an answer, notably because of the composition of Danish production and exports.

3. Exports

Danish exports increased considerably during the late 1980s, but exports grew less than overall markets. For 30 years, the share of Danish exports in OECD imports has been diminishing (Figure I.6). Despite the increased internationalisation of the 1980s, Denmark's ratio of exports to GDP did not rise after 1985, although it is still above the OECD and EU average. A high export to GDP ratio is common in small countries, as they are unable to gain the economic advantages of specialisation and economies of scale solely on the domestic market.

21

Figure 1.6. **Export of goods and services**
Denmark and the OECD

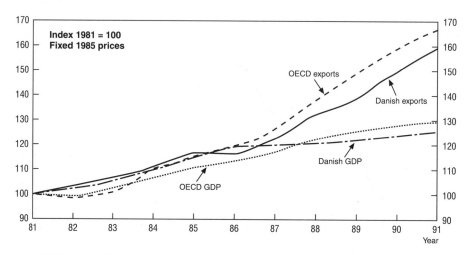

Source: OECD, *National Accounts,* 1993.

Danish exports are concentrated in a small number of nearby markets, *i.e.* there is high dependency on few markets. In terms of their content, low-technology and low-growth products play a large role (Figures I.7 and I.8). Recent analysis (Government White Paper on Trade and Industry, 1993) suggests that a slight change in the composition of exports is now occurring, with growth products in stagnating industries becoming relatively more important in Danish exports.

Because low-growth products and production dominate Danish exports, a sudden general increase in economic growth in the export markets would be of only little benefit to Danish companies and the Danish economy; the problem is exacerbated by the concentration of exports to a small number of nearby markets. In addition, the importance of low-technology products in exports means that companies, and the Danish economy, are extremely vulnerable to competition from low-cost countries, *e.g.* in Eastern Europe.

4. Social development

In the 1980s and early 1990s, Danish society saw a number of fundamental social developments. However, these are not easy to document or to quantify.

First, public opinion on Denmark's integration into the international economic and political community has evolved in the direction of greater acceptance. The most note-

Figure I.7. **Relative export specialisation**
Technological content of products

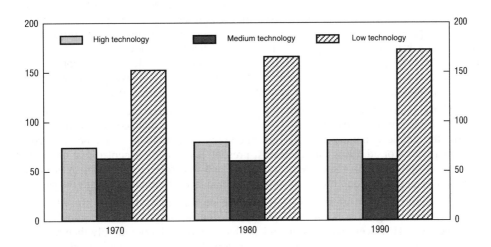

Source: OECD, 1992   Strategic Forum.

Figure I.8. **Shares of Danish industrial exports**
Low, medium and high growth

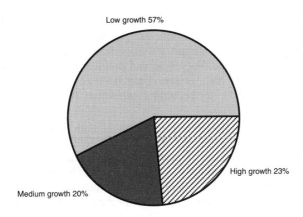

Source: Strategic Forum. Estimation based on Eurostat, *EC-Panorama 1992*, and OECD data.

worthy example is membership in the European Union, which the Danes first rejected by referendum (the Maastricht Treaty), but then accepted (the Edinburgh Treaty).

Second, public opinion on the importance of science, research, and technology has changed. In the early 1980s, public debate focused on the negative impact of technological development (for example, on the environment) and on the ethical problems of science in a way that generally discredited both technological development and science. During the 1980s, a number of institutions were established which drew attention to the balance between the costs and benefits of research and technology, so that, at present, public opinion can be described as generally positive, but critical (see Chapter IV).

Third, public attitudes towards the need to transform society from a traditional industrial society to a post-industrial service society have changed. Even in the early 1990s, the public generally felt that the unemployment problem could be reduced by lowering wages or adjusting currencies. At present, it is widely accepted that unemployment is symptomatic of a society in transition, and that solving the problem is more a question of upgrading qualifications and skills than one of simply lowering wages.

Education has also increased in importance on the political agenda. In 1980, only 27 per cent of an age cohort entered higher education, while in 1991, the figure had risen to 55 per cent. However, numbers of students have increased more rapidly than resources for educating them, and Denmark now ranks below the OECD average in total *per capita* expenditure for education (OECD, *Education at a Glance*, 1993). The massive rise in student numbers has caused a number of adjustment problems at most educational institutions.

5.   The challenges of internationalisation

As economic and political integration increases both regionally and globally, countries face new challenges to their STI policies. The STI infrastructures become increasingly important for attracting economic activities from abroad as well as for fostering new economic activities at home. Economic and political barriers to international mobility of capital, labour, goods and services keep decreasing, leaving countries such as Denmark with no alternative to becoming attractive home bases for value-added activities.

The Danish STI system must face the challenges both of internationalisation and of the two huge and interrelated problems of the Danish economy: unemployment and the composition of production/exports. Recent studies have argued that Denmark has some unique opportunities for developing new industries which combine the production of services and commodities in areas where Danish demand is in advance with respect to that of other industrialised countries. Examples are the environment, health care, services for the elderly, and child care, which are linked to the concept and status of welfare in Denmark.

Developing these industries means first creating an advanced infrastructure, but it also involves creating specific and even more advanced demand for new concepts that integrate services and manufactured products, educational systems, etc. An appropriate infrastructure in specific areas related to the welfare concept will both foster new industries and companies, and thus employment and export, and also attract foreign investment for setting up production facilities in these areas. The STI system obviously has a role to play in the formation of an attractive home base for the new welfare industries.

Being an attractive home base, however, involves some conflicting challenges. First, it implies being specialised, unique, and internationally-competitive in specific areas. Developing such specialisations involves a certain concentration of resources and activities. Second, it implies a range of STI capabilities, since STI is becoming increasingly multi-disciplinary and since, over time, changes in focus and complexity will be needed. Third, core activities and capabilities must be located in the country in such a way that they attract economic activities, rather than allowing economic activities to attract the STI activities and capabilities to their location. Fourth, international competitiveness in STI activities implies a high level of mobility of researchers, etc., and a high level of international STI co-operation in general.

II. THE DANISH STI SYSTEM: MAIN INDICATORS

As an introduction to the following chapters on the STI system, this chapter presents some key figures concerning Danish R&D and innovation. They concern the total Danish research effort (Section 1), public research (Section 2), research in the business enterprise sector (Section 3), as well as data on the innovativeness of Danish industry. Unfortunately, data, other than R&D data, on science, technology, and innovation, are scarce and often not internationally-comparable; a problem that concerns not only Denmark but all OECD countries.

1. The overall Danish R&D effort

Gross expenditure on R&D increased considerably during the 1980s and amounted to DKr 14 100 million in 1991. In fact, the compound annual growth rate, in constant prices, has increased more in Denmark than in most other OECD countries.

Nevertheless, after decades of being a below-average spender on R&D, a country does not become a top spender in relative terms overnight (Table II.1). When R&D expenditure is measured as a percentage of GDP, Denmark is still below both the European Union (EU) and the Nordic country average. As late as 1991, Denmark spent 1.59 per cent of GDP on R&D when the EU average was 1.96 per cent, that of the Nordic countries, 2.12 per cent, and that of Germany, Japan, Sweden, and the United States over 2.5 per cent. However, Denmark has surpassed Canada since 1987. The growth of gross expenditure on R&D is primarily due to the increase in business enterprise sector R&D, which amounted to DKr 8 254 million in 1991.

Table II.2 shows the rise in gross expenditure on R&D in the public and the private (business enterprise) sectors since 1981, when gross expenditure on R&D was equally divided among the public and the private sectors. The index for gross expenditure on R&D reached 314 in 1991, while that of private sector R&D was 369, against 260 for the public sector. As a result of the differences in growth rates, gross expenditure in 1991 was unevenly divided: 41 per cent in the public sector and 59 per cent in the private sector (Table II.3).

In 1991, DKr 5 846 million were spent on R&D in the public sector in Denmark. The majority of this R&D was performed at institutions of higher education (54 per cent),

Table II.1.   **Gross expenditures on R&D as a percentage of GDP**

(percentages, 1986-91)

	1986	1987	1988	1989	1990	1991
Austria	1.31	1.32	1.36	1.37	1.40	1.48
Belgium	1.68	1.68	1.64	1.69	1.69	n.a.
Canada	1.47	1.42	1.37	1.36	1.44	1.46
Denmark	1.32	1.42	1.49	1.54	n.a.	1.59
Finland	1.67	1.73	1.77	1.80	1.87	n.a.
France	2.23	2.27	2.28	2.33	2.42	2.42
Germany	2.73	2.88	2.86	2.87	2.73	2.58
Iceland	0.73	0.77	n.a.	1.03	1.03	1.02
Ireland	0.89	0.87	0.85	0.86	0.90	n.a.
Italy	1.13	1.19	1.22	1.24	1.30	1.38
Japan	2.75	2.82	2.86	2.98	3.07	3.04
Netherlands	2.22	2.33	2.26	2.16	2.06	2.00
Norway	n.a.	1.82	n.a.	1.86	n.a.	1.83
Portugal	0.45	n.a.	0.50	n.a.	0.61	n.a.
Spain	0.61	0.64	0.72	0.75	0.85	0.87
Sweden	n.a.	3.00	n.a.	2.85	n.a.	2.54
Switzerland	2.88	n.a.	n.a.	2.86	n.a.	n.a.
Turkey	0.64	0.53	0.13	0.14	0.47	n.a.
United Kingdom	2.33	2.24	2.20	2.23	2.22	n.a.
United States	2.91	2.87	2.84	2.80	2.77	2.78
EU	1.93	1.96	1.96	1.99	1.99	1.96
Nordic countries	n.a.	2.14	n.a.	2.14	n.a.	2.12

Source: OECD, *Main Science and Technology Indicators, 1993: 1.*

Table II.2.   **Gross expenditures on R&D in Denmark by main sectors of performance**

(1981-91)

	Public sector	Private sector	Total
1981	100	100	100
1982	113	123	118
1983	127	146	136
1984	140	168	154
1985	153	190	172
1986	175	219	197
1987	196	247	222
1988	217	270	243
1989	238	293	265
1990	249	331	290
1991	260	369	314

Note: Index 1981 = 100.
Source: Ministry of Research and Technology, *Forskning og udviklingsarbejde i den offentlige sektor 1991*, Copenhagen 1992.

Table II.3.   **Gross expenditures on R&D in Denmark by main sectors of performance**

(percentage distribution, 1981-91)

	Public sector	Private sector	Total
1981	50	50	100
1982	48	52	100
1983	47	53	100
1984	46	54	100
1985	45	55	100
1986	45	55	100
1987	44	56	100
1988	45	55	100
1989	45	55	100
1990	43	57	100
1991	41	59	100

Source: Ministry of Research and Technology, *Forskning og udviklingsarbejde i den offentlige sektor 1991*, Copenhagen 1992.

while government research institutes accounted for 43 per cent and private non-profit R&D institutions for only 3 per cent of public sector R&D.

Table II.4 identifies the evolution of R&D expenditures since 1981 for each of the three sub-sectors. Private non-profit R&D institutions have increased their R&D spending the most (an index of 418 in 1991). Government research institutes, on the other hand, have increased their R&D expenditures the least (an index of 246 in 1991). R&D performance, as measured by numbers of R&D personnel, shows the same evolution.

Table II.4.   **Public sector expenditure on R&D (PERD) by sector of performance, in current prices**

(million DKr, 1981-91)

	Institutions of higher education	Government research institutions	Private non-profit R&D institutions	Total
1981	100	100	100	100
1982	113	114	108	113
1983	128	125	125	127
1984	142	137	145	140
1985	157	148	163	153
1986	178	169	215	175
1987	198	190	268	196
1988	223	207	303	217
1989	247	223	335	238
1990	257	235	375	249
1991	266	246	418	260

Note: Index 1981 = 100.
Source: Ministry of Research and Technology, *Forskning og udviklingsarbejde i den offentlige sektor 1991*, Copenhagen 1992.

In 1991, there were 10 514 R&D personnel, in full-time equivalents, in the public sector. Institutions of higher education performed 55 per cent, government research institutes, 42 per cent, and private non-profit R&D institutions, the remaining 3 per cent.

2. Public R&D expenditure

Denmark's public sector R&D is relatively impressive in comparison to that of other industrialised countries. Table II.5 presents an international comparison of public sector R&D, divided between R&D performed at institutions of higher education (HERD) and R&D performed at government research institutes (GOVRD).

Denmark's HERD has been increasing as a percentage of GDP. In 1981, it was 0.32, and it has increased steadily to 0.38 in 1991. The EU average is only 0.33, although it has also been increasing since 1981. While the figures for countries such as Norway, Sweden, and the Netherlands are higher, a comparison of HERD growth rates gives a picture of convergence, since HERD has increased more in Denmark than in most other countries.

GOVRD has increased less than HERD and does not exceed the EU average. As a percentage of GDP, GOVRD increased from 0.26 in 1981 to 0.30 in 1991 but remains below the EU average of 0.36. Since government research institutions play a very different role in Sweden's STI structure, Danish GOVRD/GDP exceeds the Nordic average as well, but it is somewhat lower than Norway's alone.

Table II.6 compares the three sub-sectors not to GDP, but to gross domestic R&D. It shows that the share of institutions of higher education and government research institutes in the national total has decreased since 1986, with the former dropping from 24.1 to 22.6 per cent, and the latter from 19.5 to 17.7 per cent, essentially due to a strong increase in business sector R&D.

Second, the table shows that institutions of higher education play a larger role in national R&D in Denmark than they do, on average, in the EU, where the average share of institutions of higher education in total national R&D also increased from 1986 to 1991, but reached only 16.5 per cent in 1990. However, institutions of higher education play a larger role in Norway and Sweden than in Denmark, with 26.8 and 33.0 per cent, respectively, in 1991.

In relative terms, government research institutions apparently play the same role in Denmark as in most EU countries. Although R&D performed by government research institutes has increased as a share of total R&D in the EU, while it has decreased in Denmark, the share of GOVRD in Gross Domestic R&D in Denmark is still close to the EU average. In countries such as Japan, the United States, and particularly Sweden, government research institutes play a far smaller role in total national R&D than in Denmark.

Private non-profit R&D institutions apparently play a minor role in all countries analysed.

Table II.5. **Public sector R&D by sector of performance**
International comparison

	1986	1987	1988	1989	1990	1991
Denmark						
HERD/GDP[1]	0.32	0.34	0.36	0.38	0.38	0.38
HERD growth[2]	8.6	6.7	8.5	6.3		
GOVRD/GDP[3]	0.26	0.28	0.29	0.29	0.30	0.30
GOVRD growth[4]	9.2	7.3	5.2	3.6		
Norway						
HERD/GDP		0.39		0.45		0.49
HERD growth		1.3		7.7		6.6
GOVRD/GDP		0.29		0.36		0.34
GOVRD growth		8.5				−1.4
Sweden						
HERD/GDP		0.87		0.91		0.84
HERD growth		7.3		4.7		−4.4
GOVRD/GDP		0.13		0.11		0.10
GOVRD growth		2.3		−2.8		−8.9
Nordic average						
HERD/GDP		0.55		0.58		
HERD growth		6.6		5.3		
GOVRD/GDP		0.24		0.25		
GOVRD growth		7.3		3.7		
Netherlands						
HERD/GDP	0.49	0.50	0.47	0.46	0.48	
HERD growth	2.5	3.0	−3.7	3.0	8.3	
GOVRD/GDP	0.38	0.40	0.39	0.37	0.37	
GOVRD growth	2.1	6.2	−1.3	0.3	3.5	
United Kingdom						
HERD/GDP	0.33	0.33	0.32	0.32	0.33	
HERD growth	5.5	4.3	1.3	0.0	3.9	
GOVRD/GDP	0.36	0.32	0.32	0.33	0.31	
GOVRD growth		−6.0	2.2	5.6	−4.4	
EU-average						
HERD/GDP	0.30	0.32	0.32	0.32	0.33	
HERD growth	3.6		3.5	4.1	5.7	
GOVRD/GDP	0.34	0.35	0.34	0.35	0.35	0.36
GOVRD growth		3.7	2.6	4.5	3.3	
Japan						
HERD/GDP	0.55	0.56	0.54	0.54	0.54	0.53
HERD growth	0.6	6.8	2.5	3.8	5.6	2.9
GOVRD/GDP	0.25	0.27	0.25	0.24	0.23	0.23
GOVRD growth	1.8	12.2	−1.2	0.1	0.3	5.2
United States						
HERD/GDP	0.40	0.42	0.42	0.43	0.44	0.46
HERD growth	9.8	8.5	5.8	5.6	3.1	2.4
GOVRD/GDP	0.33	0.31	0.30	0.30	0.30	0.31
GOVRD growth	−0.1	−3.9	3.0	1.9	1.7	1.1

1. Higher Education Expenditure on R&D (HERD) as % of GDP.
2. HERD – compound annual growth rate (constant prices).
3. Government Research Institutions expenditure on R&D (GOVRD) as % of GDP.
4. GOVRD – compound annual growth rate (constant prices). 1986-91 in %.
Source: OECD, *Main Science and Technology Indicators, 1993: 1,* Paris 1993.

Table II.6. **Public sector R&D by sector of performance**
International comparison
Share of gross domestic R&D

(percentages, 1986-91)

	1986	1987	1988	1989	1990	1991
Denmark						
HERD	24.1	23.9	24.4	24.8	23.6	22.6
Government	19.5	19.4	19.2	19.1	18.3	17.7
Private	1.0	1.1	1.1	1.1	1.1	1.2
Norway						
HERD	n.a.	21.2	n.a.	24.0	n.a.	26.8
Government	n.a.	15.8	n.a.	19.4	n.a.	18.5
Private	n.a.	1.0	n.a.	n.a.	n.a.	n.a.
Sweden						
HERD	n.a.	28.9	n.a.	31.8	n.a.	33.0
Government	n.a.	4.2	n.a.	4.0	n.a.	3.8
Private	n.a.	0.1	n.a.	0.1	n.a.	0.1
Nordic average						
HERD	n.a.	25.6	27.2	27.2	n.a.	n.a.
Government	n.a.	11.1	11.5	11.5	n.a.	n.a.
Private	n.a.	0.5	n.a.	n.a.	n.a.	n.a.
Netherlands						
HERD	22.0	21.4	20.7	21.4	23.5	n.a.
Government	17.2	17.3	17.2	17.3	18.1	n.a.
Private	2.3	2.1	2.1	2.1	2.2	n.a.
United Kingdom						
HERD	14.3	14.8	14.7	14.2	14.7	n.a.
Government	15.4	14.4	14.3	14.7	14.0	n.a.
Private	3.8	3.7	4.0	4.2	4.6	n.a.
EU-average						
HERD	15.7	16.2	16.1	16.0	16.5	n.a.
Government	17.8	17.6	17.4	17.4	17.4	18.5
Private	1.5	1.4	1.5	1.5	1.6	n.a.
Japan						
HERD	19.9	19.9	19.0	18.0	17.6	17.5
Government	9.1	9.6	8.8	8.1	7.5	7.6
Private	4.4	4.5	4.3	4.2	4.1	4.2
United States						
HERD	13.7	14.5	14.9	15.5	16.0	16.4
Government	11.4	10.7	10.7	10.8	11.0	11.1
Private	2.8	2.7	2.6	2.8	3.1	3.3

Source: OECD, *Main Science and Technology Indicators, 1993: 1,* Paris 1993.

3.   R&D in the business enterprise sector

Research and development activities (R&D) in the business enterprise sector are performed by enterprises in primary industries; enterprises in manufacturing; enterprises in the service industries (including transport, construction, trade, business services, welfare and consumer services); and technological service institutes (the Approved Technological Service Institutes' [ATSI] scheme and service institutes serving the primary industries).

As innovation activities are not currently included in the statistics, the description of the development of STI activities given here covers only R&D, so that overall STI activities may be underestimated. Some studies show that innovation and R&D costs constitute around 50 per cent of all STI costs and that innovation costs are not necessarily proportional to the R&D costs. While the focus on R&D is a pragmatic necessity due to the limitations of the statistics, most STI activities in the business enterprise sector are concerned with R&D rather than innovation as a whole. However, technological service institutes emphasize non-R&D activities, such as training, testing, and consulting.

The issue of how to support business enterprise development in general and how to quantify not only R&D activities but also other innovation activities, requires further study.

Increasing business sector R&D

In 1991, the most recent year for which the Ministry of Research and Technology has figures on R&D efforts, business enterprise R&D (BERD) amounted to DKr 8.3 billion, or the R&D work of 15 200 full-time scientists and researchers. In that year, business enterprises R&D accounted for 59 per cent of total Danish R&D expenditure, a share which has risen constantly from 50 per cent in 1981 (Table II.3). Its three sub-sectors have developed somewhat differently since 1981, and, at present, manufacturing enterprises account for 70.4 per cent of BERD, service enterprises for 21.1 per cent, and the technological service institutes for 8.5 per cent.

The index of R&D expenditure for manufacturing has risen by only 322 between 1981 and 1991, while that of service enterprises show the most impressive growth – an index of 900 in terms of expenditures and of 375 in terms of R&D personnel. The technological service institutes have lagged behind average growth in the business enterprises sector, most notably during the first half of the 1980s, but in recent years, they have regained some of their share of the business enterprise sector total. At present, BERD is 0.99 per cent of GDP, against only 0.55 per cent in 1981.

The increase in BERD is impressive. Table II.7 traces the evolution of BERD in Denmark and in six other industrialised countries: Norway, Sweden, the Netherlands, the United Kingdom, Japan and the United States. Calculated in constant prices, the index of BERD in Denmark rose by 132 between 1981 and 1991. Only Japan showed greater growth (index of 141). In the United States, BERD stagnated, barely exceeding the 1981

Table II.7. Business enterprise expenditure on R&D [1]
(1986-91)

	1986	1987	1988	1989	1990	1991
Denmark						
BERD, constant prices	500	540	570	593	656	712
Index 1987 = 100	93	100	106	110	121	132
Norway						
BERD, constant prices	n.a.	566	n.a.	529	n.a.	521
Index 1987 = 100	n.a.	100	n.a.	93	n.a.	92
Sweden						
BERD, constant prices	n.a.	2 285	n.a.	2 180	n.a.	1 898
Index 1987 = 100	n.a.	100	n.a.	95	n.a.	83
Netherlands						
BERD, constant prices	2 245	2 401	2 419	2 377	2 228	2 179
Index 1987 = 100	94	100	101	99	93	91
United Kingdom						
BERD, constant prices	10 493	10 638	10 902	11 250	11 208	10 072
Index 1987 = 100	99	100	102	106	105	95
Japan						
BERD, constant prices	27 279	28 940	32 052	35 886	39 551	40 815
Index 1987 = 100	94	100	111	124	137	141
United States						
BERD, constant prices	85 980	87 594	90 062	90 258	88 816	87 622
Index 1987 = 100	98	100	103	103	101	100

1. Million constant US$ (1985 prices and PPPs).
Source: OECD, *Basic Science and Technology Indicators Statistics,* Paris 1993.

level in 1991 (constant prices). In Norway, Sweden, the United Kingdom, and the Netherlands, BERD has decreased in constant prices, especially since 1988 or 1989, and is now below the 1981 level.

Low R&D spending

Compared to most other countries, the Danish business enterprise sector is still a low-spender on R&D. Only five out of 16 OECD countries spend less on BERD as a percentage of GDP (Table II.8). On the other hand, the percentage has decreased dramatically in most OECD countries over the past decade. In addition to Denmark, Japan, France, and Italy are exceptions.

Table II.8. **BERD as a percentage of GDP in 17 OECD countries**

(1986-91)

	1986	1987	1988	1989	1990	1991
Japan	1.83	1.86	1.94	2.08	2.18	2.15
Switzerland	2.24	n.a.	n.a.	2.14	n.a.	n.a.
Germany	2.00	2.08	2.07	2.07	1.95	1.76
United States	2.10	2.07	2.04	1.98	1.94	1.92
Sweden	n.a.	2.00	n.a.	1.82	n.a.	1.61
France	1.31	1.34	1.35	1.41	1.46	1.48
United Kingdom	1.55	1.50	1.47	1.49	1.48	1.36
Netherlands	1.30	1.38	1.36	1.28	1.16	1.11
Norway	n.a.	1.13	n.a.	1.05	n.a.	1.00
Finland	0.98	1.02	1.06	1.11	1.17	n.a.
Belgium	1.21	1.23	1.21	1.22	1.23	n.a.
Denmark	0.73	0.79	0.82	0.85	n.a.	0.99
Canada	0.80	0.79	0.77	0.74	0.77	0.78
Italy	0.66	0.68	0.70	0.73	0.76	0.77
Austria	n.a.	n.a.	n.a.	0.80	n.a.	n.a.
Australia	0.48	0.49	0.53	0.53	0.53	n.a.
Iceland	n.a.	0.12	n.a.	0.20	0.20	0.20

Source: OECD, *Main Science and Technology Indicators, 1993: 1,* Paris 1993.

Its low R&D intensity has caused some concern in Denmark. This situation has three different causes. The first is the relative size of the Danish business enterprise sector compared to that of other countries. When BERD is examined as percentage of domestic product of industry (DPI) instead of GDP, as in Table II.9, R&D intensity increases in Denmark from 1.13 per cent in 1981 to 1.49 per cent in 1991. Here again, R&D intensity decreases in most other OECD countries from 1987-88, except for Japan, France, Italy, and, in this calculation, Finland as well. While R&D intensity in the Danish business enterprise sector is moving towards the OECD average, it still remains below it.

The second cause of the low R&D intensity is the industrial composition of the business enterprise sector, which has a large share of manufacturing of agricultural products. Since this is not an R&D-intensive sector in any country, the composition of the Danish business enterprise sector naturally leads to low average R&D intensity when compared to countries with an industrial structure. Nevertheless, individual industries might be expected to perform as much R&D *per capita* as identical industries in other advanced countries. However, as Table II.10 shows, this is not the case. Even for foodstuffs, countries such as Sweden and Japan perform more R&D *per capita* (here measured as value added) than Denmark.

The Danish pharmaceuticals industry is very competitive and performs a large share of total BERD. However, the pharmaceuticals industry in Sweden, Finland, Norway, the United Kingdom, and Germany performs more R&D (again measured as value added)

Table II.9. BERD as a percentage of DPI in 14 OECD countries

(1986-91)

	1986	1987	1988	1989	1990	1991
Japan	2.05	2.07	2.15	2.30	2.40	n.a.
Germany	2.52	2.63	2.61	2.60	2.44	2.41
United States	2.38	2.35	2.29	2.23	n.a.	n.a.
Sweden	n.a.	3.00	n.a.	2.72	n.a.	n.a.
France	1.75	1.78	1.79	1.85	1.92	1.94
United Kingdom	2.19	2.13	2.07	2.10	2.08	n.a.
Netherlands	1.65	1.77	1.73	1.61	1.45	n.a.
Norway	n.a.	1.55	n.a.	n.a.	1.42	n.a.
Finland	1.38	1.44	1.51	1.57	1.68	n.a.
Belgium	1.56	1.57	1.54	1.54	1.54	n.a.
Denmark	1.13	1.23	1.28	1.30	1.40	1.49
Canada	1.10	1.08	1.05	1.02	n.a.	n.a.
Italy	0.81	0.83	0.87	0.90	0.94	n.a.
Australia	0.51	0.52	0.55	0.56	0.56	n.a.

Source: OECD, *Main Science and Technology Indicators, 1993: 1,* Paris 1993.

than in Denmark. Japan's pharmaceutical industry is the only one less R&D-intensive than Denmark's (Table II.10).

The R&D intensity of Danish industries is low, when compared to that of the other countries analysed, with the sole exception of the manufacturing of measuring instruments.

Table II.10. R&D intensity in industry
Intramural R&D expenditures as a percentage of value added

(1987)

	Denmark	Sweden	Finland	Norway	United Kingdom	Japan	Germany
Food stuff	1.1	1.8	1.0	0.4	0.9	1.7	0.5
Pharmaceutical	15.7	35.0	27.8	22.1	19.4	12.7	19.6
Chemical industry	2.3	2.9	4.6	4.1	4.0	5.7	4.6
Machinery industry	5.1	11.6	5.4	4.3	2.4	4.1	5.7
Electronic industry	8.3	19.1	15.8	16.6	17.3	13.4	12.1
Transport equipment	2.3	14.6	4.5	1.6	3.7	10.1	7.0
Instruments	16.2	13.4	16.8	47.0	5.9	12.3	5.8

Source: Ministry of Education, 1991.

The third reason hinges on the composition of the Danish industry according to size of companies. Table II.11 compares Denmark in this respect to the other Nordic countries. It shows that average BERD per employee increases with size of company (measured by number of employees). It also reveals that the percentage share of small companies (less than 50 employees) is high in Denmark (second to Norway), and that that of large companies (more than 500 employees) is small (33 per cent compared to 37 per cent in Finland and 53 per cent in Sweden). This is evidence that the size of Danish companies at least partly explains the low average R&D intensity of the business enterprise sector. On the other hand, Table II.11 also shows that BERD per employee is higher in small companies in Denmark than in small companies in other Nordic countries. BERD per employee in large companies is still smaller than BERD per employee in large companies of other Nordic countries.

Table II.11. **BERD expenditures and total employment in the Business Enterprise Sector in Denmark, Finland, Norway and Sweden distributed according to the size of companies**

(number of employees, 1989)

Firm size	Denmark	Finland	Norway	Sweden
Share of BERD-expenditures (%)				
0-50	10	3	11	1
50-90	5	2	7	2
100-199	9	2	8	2
200-499	15	5	12	5
500+	61	88	62	90
Share of BERD-employment (%)				
0-50	23	19	31	17
50-90	12	7	16	12
100-199	13	8	16	14
200-499	19	13	18	20
500+	33	53	19	37
Average BERD/employee (1 000 SKr)				
0-50	5 000	2 000	4 000	1 000
50-90	5 000	4 000	5 000	4 000
100-199	8 000	3 000	5 000	4 000
200-499	9 000	5 000	7 000	6 000
500+	21 000	22 000	35 000	61 000
Total	11 000	14 000	12 000	25 000

Source: Nordisk Industrifond, *Vitenskaps- og teknologiindikatorer for Norden,* 1992.

4. Innovation expenditures

As discussed so far, the STI system primarily concerns the R&D aspects of innovation. Less attention has been paid to other activities of the institutes, such as training, consulting, etc., which facilitate innovation in firms. This section deals with innovative activities on the basis of data from the two innovation surveys that have been taken in Denmark. The first is the Nordic Innovation Survey carried out in 1989-90 in four Nordic countries; the second, held in 1993-94 under the auspices of the European Union, covered all EU countries.

While the Nordic Innovation Survey covered a small sample (600 enterprises in Denmark) of firms investing in R&D, the 1993 survey covered a large representative sample of all Danish firms with over 20 employees. Unfortunately, the latter results are not yet internationally comparable. The data from the 1993 survey used in this report are taken from Christensen and Kristensen (1994) [*Innovationsaktiviteter i Dansk industri* by Jesper L. Christensen and Arne Kristensen (version 15.7.1994)].

Technology and innovation are not a question of R&D alone. As Figure II.1 indicates, less than half of all costs associated with innovation are R&D costs. Other important aspects of total innovation costs are trial production (27 per cent) and product design (16 per cent).

Table II.12 compares the breakdown of innovation costs in various countries. The percentages differ somewhat from the 1993 survey figures in Figure II.1. The earlier survey is likely to overestimate the importance of R&D to innovation, since it sampled R&D performing companies. Innovative companies that do not perform R&D were excluded from the earlier survey. In some sense, this indicates that for some industries and companies, the STI system, as identified in this report, is not closely related to innovation.

R&D plays a smaller role in overall innovation in Denmark than in Norway, but a larger role than in Finland. As Table II.12 shows, R&D accounts for two-thirds of total innovation costs in Norway's manufacturing industry but only half in Denmark's. On the other hand, implementation and marketing play a larger role in Denmark than in the other two countries, while equipment costs dominate in Finnish manufacturing industry.

This can be explained in part by the composition of industries. Table II.13 breaks down total innovation costs by aspects of innovation and industries. It shows that in Denmark, R&D plays a far smaller role in innovation in the dominant foodstuffs industry (8 per cent) than it does in Norway (42 per cent) and Finland (41 per cent). In Denmark, 52 per cent of total innovation costs in the foodstuffs industry are associated with marketing. In Norway and Finland, innovation costs are strongly associated with equipment.

Innovation costs are measured only for companies, and one peculiarity of the Danish foodstuffs industry is the role played both by government development stations and by common industry research facilities, which focus on process R&D. In fact, the breakdown of the industry's innovation costs points to the importance of these actors as an important factor in explaining the low R&D intensity of the business enterprise sector. It also emphasizes the importance of a fully-functioning STI system.

Figure II.1. **Innovation expenditures**
Danish Innovation Survey 1993

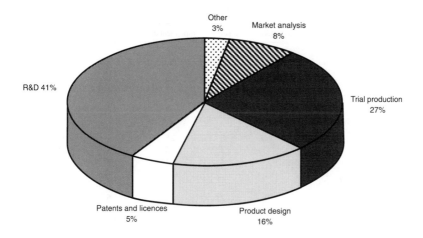

Source: Innovationsaktiviteter i Dansk Industri.

Table II.12.   **Total innovation costs in manufacturing industry in 1988
divided among R&D, patents, implementation, marketing and equipment
Denmark, Norway and Finland**

(percentages)

	R&D	Patents	Implementation	Marketing	Equipment	Total
Denmark	51	5	14	13	17	100
Norway	67	3	10	10	10	100
Finland	40	5	6	5	44	100

Source: Nordisk Industrifond, *Innovation Activities in the Nordic Countries,* Oslo 1991.

Table II.13. **Total innovation costs in manufacturing industry in 1988 divided among R&D, patents, implementation, marketing and equipment, industries and countries**

(percentages)

	R&D	Patents	Implementation	Marketing	Equipment	Total
Foodstuff industry						
Norway	42	0	6	8	44	100
Finland	41	9	7	8	35	100
Denmark	8	10	23	52	7	100
Textile and furniture industry						
Norway	60	0	25	1	14	100
Finland	45	13	6	8	28	100
Denmark	53	4	3	6	34	100
Wood, paper and pulp industry						
Norway	76	2	4	5	13	100
Finland	10	1	4	4	81	100
Denmark	17	2	10	11	60	100
Chemical industry						
Norway	76	2	4	11	7	100
Finland	86	4	2	3	5	100
Denmark	82	2	2	3	11	100
Iron and metal industry						
Norway	73	2	9	8	8	100
Finland	48	8	12	4	28	100
Denmark	57	2	16	11	14	100
Machinery and transport equipment industry						
Norway	59	3	13	12	13	100
Finland	55	9	9	4	23	100
Denmark	51	7	17	14	12	100
Electronics industry						
Norway	67	3	12	10	8	100
Finland	62	5	6	10	16	100
Denmark	67	3	10	12	8	100
Electrical machinery industry						
Norway	55	5	14	13	13	100
Finland	80	8	7	4	1	100
Denmark	40	3	10	14	33	100
Manufacturing industry n.m.e.						
Norway	63	2	12	11	12	100
Finland	27	7	5	6	55	100
Denmark	44	6	10	6	33	100

Source: Nordisk Industrifond, *Innovation Activities in the Nordic Countries,* Oslo 1991.

Enterprises can be grouped not only according to industry and size, but also according to the main characteristics of their innovation process. Using Pavitt's (1984) classification of four types of innovation, Fakstorp (1993) attempted to quantify (by value of production) the distribution of Danish manufacturing industry. He found the following shares: supplier-dominated (55 per cent); economy-of-scale intensive (16 per cent); specialised suppliers (16 per cent); technology-based R&D (13 per cent). While the method used for quantification seems questionable, the typology has also been used by Christensen (1994) in a fruitful attempt to describe the innovation process in Danish industries and trade.

III. CO-ORDINATION OF THE DANISH STI SYSTEM

This chapter, which describes the Danish STI system and the recent changes at the ministerial and policy advisory level, has three main sections. The first deals with the ministerial structure, the second with the advisory structure, and the third with the national evaluations. The section dealing with the advisory structure is sub-divided into three parts, devoted to the national research councils, the Danish Council for Research Policy, and the Industry and Trade Development Council. The chapter concludes that both the present ministerial structure and the high-level advisory structure require further consideration.

By way of introduction, it is worth recalling that the 1987 OECD review of the Danish STI system recommended strengthening the high-level policy-making bodies of the Danish STI system. It made several specific proposals. It suggested that a committee, chaired by the Prime Minister, should be established in order to give the government a more coherent overview of S&T policy and to strengthen interministerial co-ordination, and that a new high-level committee from industry should advise the Minister of Education on university research. It further suggested that the Technical Research Council and the Agricultural and Veterinary Research Council should be combined with corresponding councils under the Ministries of Industry and Agriculture. Finally, it recommended strengthening the advisory function of the research councils and their administrative secretariat and granting them greater independence.

These specific recommendations have been followed only to a certain extent. No high-level committee chaired by the Prime Minister has been established. In 1988, the Government Committee on Research was established; it was dissolved in 1993 and re-established in March 1994. No high-level committee from industry has been formed to advise the Minister of Education on university research. However, the Danish Council for Research Policy, among others, advises the Minister of Education, and it is composed of industry representatives as well as representatives of government research institutes, universities, etc. In practice, the Council has up to now been headed by an industrialist.

The Technical Research Council and the Agricultural and Veterinary Research Council have not been combined with corresponding councils under the Ministries of Industry and of Agriculture. However, joint strategic R&D programmes have been implemented (see Chapter IV).

Finally, the advisory function of the national research councils has not been strengthened, although their administrative secretariat has become more independent, without, however, any increase in their resources.

The founding of the Danish Council for Policy Research was designed, in principle, to strengthen the cross-disciplinary and cross-sectoral advisory function. Yet the advisory structure remains somewhat dispersed, with, in practice, no clear division of roles between the national research councils and the Danish Council for Research Policy. High-level policy for the STI system has been strengthened by the creation of the Ministry of Research, by major national evaluations, and by the strategic STI programmes.

1.   The ministerial structure

Historically, ministerial responsibility for science, technology and innovation in Denmark has been shared among the Ministry of Education, responsible for science in the institutions of higher education, the Ministry of Industry, responsible for science, technology and innovation in the business enterprise sector, including the technological service institutes, and other ministries, such as Agriculture, Housing, and Environment, responsible for the STI activities of ''their own'' government research institutes.

In 1988, the Ministry of Education became the Ministry of Education and Research. Politically, this was seen as a way to give STI policy higher priority in overall government policy, and also as a way to upgrade the status of the Minister for Education at that time, who had demonstrated a keen interest in STI policy and, primarily, in internationalising the STI system by increasing Danish participation in the EU Framework Programmes in research, technology and development.

The change of name did not in fact change ministerial responsibilities, and the upgrading of STI policy within both the ministry and the government could have taken place within the old Ministry of Education. Nevertheless, the change provided an occasion for taking a number of initiatives to strengthen STI policy.

First, a Government Committee on Research was formed, headed by the Minister for Education and Research. The mere existence of this committee improved interministerial co-ordination of research policy at the administrative level, as became evident when the Committee was dissolved from 1993 to March 1994.

Second, within the Ministry, the Danish Research Administration, which had been a secretariat, became a directorate, with the director becoming a member of the corporate board of the Ministry.

Third, a number of new STI policy initiatives were launched: an annual strategic state R&D budget, an annual white paper to the Parliament on STI policy, and the launching of cross-ministerial strategic R&D programmes.

According to interviewees, the new STI policy initiatives have improved overall co-ordination to some extent, although they still lack political force when compared to similar initiatives in other countries. The annual white paper to the Parliament on STI policy, for example, is criticised for its lack of vision, target groups, key success factors, and relevant action plans.

In 1993 the previous government, a coalition headed by liberal Poul Schlüter (Conservative), was replaced by a coalition government headed by Social Democrat Poul Nyrup Rasmussen. With the new government came a restructuring of the STI system.

First, a Ministry of Research and Technology was formed with overall responsibility for strengthening and co-ordinating Danish STI policy. Furthermore, the functions of the Ministry were extended to include the initiation and evaluation of measures in the areas of research and technology. Second, the Government Committee on Research was suppressed, as the new government wished to reduce the number of ministerial committees.

The Ministry had a total budget of about DKr 1.1 billion and was made responsible for the national research councils, for the Council for Research Policy, and for Danish participation in international research. Eleven smaller research institutions formerly under the responsibility of the Ministry of Education and Research were placed under its responsibility, as was the large research center, Risø, formerly under the Ministry of Energy, with a budget of DKr 430 million.

According to interviewees close to the political decision-making process, the political basis for founding the new ministry was not least a need to have more ministries and ministerial appointments to distribute among the four parties forming the coalition government. Few tasks were transferred from other ministries to the new Ministry of Research and Technology.

The Government Research Committee headed by the Minister of Education and Research was replaced by the Interministerial R&D Committee whose role was to co-ordinate STI matters among ministries. This committee discussed and co-ordinated the ministries' work on areas relating to research and technology. It was composed of civil servants and representatives from the various ministries. Others were invited to participate in meetings whenever it was judged necessary.

In January 1994, the Ministry of Research and Technology became the Ministry of Research. Mr A.O. Andersen, already responsible for the Ministry of Church Affairs, was appointed minister for Research. In March 1994, a Government Committee on Research was re-established, and the Interministerial R&D Committee became a committee working in parallel to the government committee.

The political basis for the 1994 restructurings is less evident than that for the previous restructurings. Interviewees point out that re-establishing the Government Committee on Research means a political upgrading of STI policy in overall government policy. They also point out that the omission of the word "technology" means that the name better fits the content. Most persons interviewed consider that the Ministry of Research still has a rather small role in overall government STI policy. Nor do they see combining the Ministry of Research with the Ministry of Church Affairs as a way to give STI policy high political priority.

There are still 17 ministries that have R&D budgets. A number of them have their own R&D councils or committees for allocating funds and advising ministers with respect to specific STI policies. Following the 1988 white paper on government research institutes, a number of restructurings have taken place within ministries. Among others, the Ministry of Agriculture reduced its strategic programme activities by 25 per cent in 1993 and increased basic funding of its institutes by the same amount. The most important ministries funding R&D are Education, Research, Agriculture, Industry, and Culture, which allocate 75 per cent of total government R&D funds (Table III.1).

A number of persons interviewed raised the issue of how to strengthen ministerial responsibility for the STI system. One option would be for the Ministry of Research to have its financial and political responsibilities increased by taking over parts of budgets and administrative tasks from other ministries. Another would be to abolish the Ministry of Research and concentrate responsibility for all or some STI appropriations under one ministry, such as the Ministry of Education or the Ministry of Finance. The arguments for concentrating financial and political responsibilities under a Ministry of Research are discussed below. (The term ''a Ministry of Research'' refers both to the Ministry of Research and to any other ministry having overall financial and political responsibility for all or some STI appropriations.)

The Ministry of Education, as the main ministerial R&D spender, covers basic appropriations for university research as well as funds for PhD students. According to persons interviewed, it has been a deliberate policy of the Ministry of Education to allocate any increase in appropriations to strategic programmes rather than to basic appropriations, thereby effectively transferring R&D funds to strategic programmes, which are ''the money by which you can make policies''. According to interviewees, the Ministry has succeeded well in this transformation. Since the strategic programmes are administrated by the Ministry of Research (and by a number of others, as discussed below), some think that there are few R&D funds ''by which one makes policies'' left in the Ministry for Education. Basic appropriations are decided upon and divided among universities only once a year. For political reasons the distribution has so far been rather conservative.

Transferring budgets and administrative responsibilities away from the Ministry of Education to a Ministry of Research would not, according to one argument, improve the political status of such a Ministry of Research, since it would not give to the latter a real opportunity to influence decision-making with related budgets. It is also argued that

Table III.1. **Budget R&D allocations to Ministries, 1993**

(percentages)

Ministry of Education	36
Ministry of Research	22
Ministry of Agriculture	7
Ministry of Industry	5
Ministry of Culture	5
Other Ministries	25

university teaching would suffer if the production of PhDs was separated from university research and that the STI structure would diverge from the typical structure of higher education in the EU. A counterargument, discussed further in Chapter V, is that basic appropriations for research should not be distributed so conservatively among universities. Thus, the issue of basic appropriations for university research could be a research policy question and a policy item on a Ministry of Research's agenda.

On the other hand, concentrating the financial and political responsibility for all or part of the STI appropriations under the Ministry of Education would obviously cause no problems for the linkages to higher education.

With respect to government research institutes, basic appropriations as well as funds for strategic programmes are the responsibility of a number of ministries. Transferring budgets and administrative responsibilities away from these ministries could be another way to strengthen a Ministry of Research. In fact, since 1993, the present Ministry of Research already has administrative and political responsibility for a government research institute formerly the responsibility of the Ministry of Energy, the Risø National Laboratory. Risø is one of the largest government research institutes and interviewees indicate that the change of administrative responsibility has been rather successful, from the point of view of both the ministry and Risø.

Interviews in government research institutes other than the Risø National Laboratory indicate that government research institutes play a relatively weak role in national STI policy planning, not least owing to the division of administrative responsibility among a number of ministries. Government research institutes are rather dependent on their respective ministries, although changes in the governing of government research institutes and the creation of SEDIRK (the Assembly of Directors of Government Research Establishments) have increased their independence. The governing of government research institutes is discussed in greater detail in Chapter V. Here, the arguments for and against concentrating administrative responsibility under a Ministry for Research are simply summarised.

Arguments expressed in favour of concentrating administrative responsibility for government research institutes under a Ministry of Research are:

- It will strengthen the government research institutes as a whole.
- It will improve interaction and co-ordination between government research institutes and research at institutions of higher education.
- It will improve research quality in government research institutes, by producing PhDs, scientific articles for international journals subject to peer review, etc.

Arguments against concentrating the administrative responsibility for government research institutes under a Ministry of Research are:

- It will weaken links between government research institutes and their users.
- It will weaken that part of the work of government research institutes that relates to official tasks such as registration and surveillance.
- It will, in the end, weaken government research institutes overall, since political support for funding government research institutes will diminish if more stress is put on research and less on government. Interviewees state that the fundamental

political *raison d'être* for public funding of government research institutes is that the research performed will support current government policy in any field. If government research institutes do not support current government policies or if government research institutes do not take care of registration and surveillance tasks, other institutions will be founded for these purposes.

– Research quality in government research institutes can be ensured through changes in financing structures, which do not presuppose a change in ministerial responsibilities as such.

A third way to strengthen the role of a Ministry of Research for overall government STI policy would be to transfer budgets and administrative responsibilities, for example for the technological service institutes, from the Ministry of Industry to a Ministry of Research.

Such a restructuring is not, however, on the present STI political agenda. It has not been suggested by any of the decision-makers interviewed, and presumably the arguments for and against would be rather similar to those regarding the government research institutes – whatever would gained with respect to co-ordination of STI policy and strengthening of interaction with government research institutes and institutions of higher education would be counterbalanced by losses in user relations.

In conclusion, strengthening high-level STI policy co-ordination by further changes in ministerial structures is first of all a question of whether or not the responsibility of a Ministry of Research should include basic university research as well as government research institutes. Ministerial structures that include technological service institutes and co-ordinating measures such as government STI white papers can also be considered.

2. The advisory structure

Historically, the advisory structure consisted of the Council for Technological Development which advised the Ministry of Industry and played a major role in the actual allocation of funds, and the Advisory Board on Research Policy which advised the government as a whole and the Parliament, but had nothing to do with the actual allocation of funds, a task accomplished by the six national research councils for their respective fields. For the relevant ministries (Agriculture, Housing, Environment, etc.), the advisory structure varied from specific councils to committees often dominated by civil servants from the ministries. Following the 1988 White Paper on government research establishments, a number of restructurings have occurred.

The national research councils

Denmark still has six national research councils (natural sciences, agricultural and veterinary sciences, technical sciences, social sciences, the humanities, and health sciences). Each council has fifteen members, all of whom are appointed in their personal capacity by the Minister for Research. Most are active researchers and, as a body, they must cover a broad disciplinary range and ensure thorough disciplinary competence in the area.

Grants from the national research councils account for only 6 per cent of the total funding of public sector R&D, but their importance is greater than the share of total funding indicates. External funding of public sector R&D is often decisive for new activities, and it is often supplemented by the R&D-performing institutes themselves with at least an equivalent amount from their basic funding.

Table III.2 shows the evolution of the national research councils' appropriations. From 1993, strategic appropriations are included in basic appropriations. Figures for 1995, 1996, and 1997 are budget appropriations. Chapter V deals in greater detail with the relation between basic and strategic funding.

In the mid-1980s, the national research councils were criticised for being too involved with university research to be able to allocate funds on a strategic or even a qualitative basis. It was said that members of the national research councils, as representatives of their respective institutions, primarily sought to ensure that their own institution received its legitimate share of national research council funding.

However, as early as the mid-1970s – the first strategic plan was published by the Technical Research Council in 1975 – the national research councils began to formulate long-term strategic plans for their funding activity. These strategic plans, again starting with that formulated by the Technical Research Council, were developed through a bottom-up or "osmosis" process.

In response to criticism, all six research councils strengthened their strategic planning during the late 1980s and now publish long-term strategic plans every four or five years in order to ensure coherence and continuity in the development of their respective research fields. At the end of the first phase of the strategic plans (1988-92), plans for the second phase (1993-97) were launched in 1991. The national research councils now concentrate their funding in larger framework appropriation, and they administer their funding with considerable freedom of disposition from the grantees.

In 1992, the Danish Council for Research Policy evaluated the strategic plans of the national research councils and concluded that they represent a valuable tool for drawing the attention of politicians and funding authorities to important fields of high-quality research which require a special effort and that they contribute to the dynamic development of Danish research.

In 1991, for the first time, a cross-council strategic plan was published as a supplement to the individual research plans of each research council. Its goal was to emphasize the importance of cross-council scientific co-operation for seeking answers to research problems. The national research councils have successfully collaborated in various programmes, such as the Food Technology Programme I (FØTEK), the Materials Technology Programme I (MUP), and the Biotechnology Programme I (BIOTEK). The councils have been responsible, in part, for planning and administering the programmes.

The national research councils also emphasize the importance of the international dimension of research programmes and co-operate with the Danish National Research Foundation.

Table III.2. The Danish Research Councils

The Danish Natural Science Research Council
(DKr millions)

	1988	1989	1990	1991	1992	1993	1994	1995	1996	1997
Basic appropriations	47.6	57.8	60.9	62.2	63.7	107.3	120.4	127.7	147.1	143.9
Strategic appropriations	–	12.0	15.2	25.6	26.2	–	–	–	–	–
MUP	–	13.2	19.5	20.0	20.5	–	13.5	12.0	12.0	8.6
PIFT	–	–	–	–	13.5	19.0	18.7	–	–	–
FTU	–	9.4	2.4	–	–	–	–	–	–	–
Other	10.1	12.6	10.1	14.5	15.6	12.8	11.9	11.1	10.9	10.9
Total	57.7	105.0	108.1	122.3	139.5	139.1	164.5	150.8	170.0	163.4

The Danish Medical Research Council
(DKr millions)

	1988	1989	1990	1991	1992	1993	1994	1995	1996	1997
Basic appropriations	49.0	51.2	52.7	53.5	54.7	80.9	83.7	84,2	85.1	83.4
Strategic appropriations	–	–	–	12.9	13.5	–	–	–	–	–
FTU	–	4.3	1.2	–	–	–	–	–	–	–
Other	1.0	1.4	–	–	0.5	0.1	–	–	–	–
Total	50.0	56.9	53.9	66.4	68.7	81.0	83.7	84.2	85.1	83.4

The Danish Agricultural and Veterinary Research Council
(DKr millions)

	1988	1989	1990	1991	1992	1993	1994	1995	1996	1997
Basic appropriations	26.0	27.9	29.4	29.7	30.3	40.0	41.9	44.7	44.0	43.1
Strategic appropriations	–	8.0	12.2	15.8	16.2	–	–	–	–	–
PIFT	–	–	–	–	6.6	9.2	9.3	–	–	–
FTU	–	11.4	3.0	–	–	–	–	–	–	–
Other	1.5	1.3	–	–	0.6	0.2	–	–	–	–
Total	27.5	48.6	44.6	45.5	53.7	49.4	51.2	44.7	44.0	43.1

The Danish Social Science Research Council
(DKr millions)

	1988	1989	1990	1991	1992	1993	1994	1995	1996	1997
Basic appropriations	28.6	31.5	31.1	32.8	32.7	35.5	37.1	37.7	36.0	35.3
Strategic appropriations	–	3.4	0.7	4.9	5.3	–	–	–	–	–
FTU	–	–	–	–	–	–	–	–	–	–
Other	1.8	–	–	–	0.4	0.1	–	–	–	–
Total	30.4	34.9	31.8	37.7	38.4	35.6	37.1	37.7	36.0	35.3

The Danish Research Council of Humanities
(DKr millions)

Basic appropriations	31.9	34.9	34.2	35.1	35.9	61.0	62.0	63.8	64.0	60.7
Strategic appropriations	–	–	–	9.2	13.5	–	–	–	–	–
FTU	–	1.9	0.5	–	–	–	–	–	–	–
Research programmes for the Humanities	–	7.4	6.6	3.8	–	–	–	–	–	–
Other	1.8	4.5	4.6	3.6	0.7	0.6	0.5	0.5	0.5	0.5
Total	33.7	48.7	45.9	51.7	50.1	61.6	62.5	64.3	64.5	61.2

The Danish Technical Research Council
(DKr millions)

Basic appropriations	38.2	41.1	43.5	44.4	44.7	86.5	89.4	92.3	94.3	92.5
Strategic appropriations	–	15.0	25.4	26.0	26.7	–	–	–	–	–
MUP	–	21.8	31.3	32.1	33.2	–	22.5	20.0	20.0	14.4
PIFT	–	–	–	–	26.6	37.6	37.6	–	–	–
FTU	–	49.8	12.3	–	–	–	–	–	–	–
Other	2.0	1.8	–	–	0.8	0.3	–	–	–	–
Total	40.2	129.5	112.5	102.5	132.0	124.4	149.5	112.3	114.3	106.9

Source: The Danish Research Councils, 1994.

The overall aims of the collaboration between the national research councils are:
- to stimulate cross-disciplinary research;
- to create programmes that go beyond what can be done without co-ordination;
- to strengthen the Danish research communities in both the national and the international context.

The councils seek to achieve their goals by establishing projects and programmes which may supplement or be part of larger national and international strategic programmes. The idea is to encourage the research communities to form alliances and formulate projects. In formulating their strategic plans, the councils use a bottom-up procedure. Individual researchers, research groups, sub-committees, potential users, etc., are invited to present their views and ideas. This material, together with the knowledge and ideas of the council members, forms the basis for a series of discussions within the councils. The resulting strategic plans, along with specific announcements, offer the research community important guidelines for the formulation of applications. Applications are received from research alliances as well as from individual researchers and research groups. Applications within selected research fields are evaluated by expert committees and, in some instances, international referees. Finally, the individual councils vote the appropriations. Each council reserves some funds for especially-qualified projects that fall outside priority fields. The aim and content of cross-disciplinary strategic research programmes are described in Chapter IV.

The national research councils also play an important advisory role to the Government and to the Parliament.

The Danish Council for Research Policy

Until 1988, the national research councils were represented on the Advisory Board on Research Policy so that criticism of the excessively close ties between the national research councils and universities and university research was a criticism of the Advisory Board as well. Accordingly, in 1989, the Advisory Board on Research Policy was dissolved and replaced by the Danish Council for Research Policy, in order to create a body more independent of both the national research councils and the government and ministries. Chairmen of the national research councils were not members of the new council. Instead, members of the council were appointed in their personal capacity from universities, government research institutes, and the business enterprise sector. The Board has so far been headed by an industrialist.

Since its foundation, the Danish Council for Research Policy has played an important role in overall co-ordination and in high-level policy areas such as specialisation in the national STI system, the governing of government research institutes, and national evaluations of research – agriculture, health, environment, etc. – on the political agenda. At the same time, however, the national research councils still advise both the Government and the Parliament within their respective fields of science, and the Assembly of Chairmen of the National Research Councils increasingly takes initiatives and gives advice with respect to overall co-ordination of STI activities. According to persons interviewed, co-ordination between the national research councils and the Danish Council for Research Policy is in practice very limited, with the national research councils represented by only one among the 23 members of the representative body of the Danish Council for Research Policy.

Because it has a limited budget for STI policy analysis and a rather small secretariat, the impact on the STI system of the Danish Council for Research Policy is heavily dependent on the initiatives, good relations with the Minister of Research, etc., of its individual members. Indeed, the Council's impact on the development of the STI system is very dependent on its chairman as an individual.

Persons interviewed pointed out that an advisory structure that is dependent on individuals is not very stable, and some conflicts have recently been arisen between the national research councils and the Council for Research Policy, which has strongly criticised the strategic plans of the national research councils on what the national research councils considered rather unprofessional grounds. This has created some strains in the STI system.

Without taking a stand on specific issues, it is nevertheless possible to conclude that the advisory structure for high-level policy for the STI system has not reached its final form. At least some of the actors at this level do not make a clear division of labour between the national research councils and the Danish Council for Research Policy. Rather severe tensions between the two have arisen with respect to the formulation of strategic plans, and the Assembly of Chairmen of the National Research Councils has proposed to the Minister of Research that the Danish Council for Research Policy should be abolished. Some argue that an Advisory Board which includes the chairmen of the national research councils as permanent members should be re-established. Others argue against re-establishing an advisory structure which was criticised for its lack of independence from the scientific community.

Consequently, the question is whether to keep a structure with both the national research councils and the Danish Council for Research Policy advising Government and Parliament or to merge the two or to consider a third structure such as the Norwegian Council for Research.

The Industry and Trade Development Council

No current discussions suggest creating any stronger relations between the national research councils and the Danish Council for Research Policy, on the one hand, and the Industry and Trade Development Council, on the other. The latter dates back to government policy of the late 1980s, which attempted to reduce the number of advisory councils and programmes and schemes relating to STI in the business enterprise sector. At that time, the Council for Technological Development administered substantial funds which were clearly divided among programmes and schemes, partly with the political goal of making the subsidising of STI transparent, at least as regards objectives.

At the same time a number of studies and analyses, carried out both in academia and in the Ministries of Finance, Education and Research, and Industry itself, pointed to the need for a broader and more holistic view of science, technology, and innovation and business development in general.

The Minister of Industry then developed a major plan for reorganising both the ministry and its advisory bodies along more corporate lines. The restructuring plan included a rather ambitious substitute for the Council for Technological Development as well as the abolishment of a number of boards, councils, etc. The substitute was to function as a high-level "think tank" rather than as a decision-making body for grants, subsidies, etc.

At the end of 1989, when Parliament agreed on the state budget for 1990, there were large cutbacks in business sector STI subsidies in return for the general reduction in corporate taxes from 50 per cent to 40 per cent. The Minister of Industry was replaced, government policies became far less specific, and there were far fewer subsidies. Instead, emphasis was placed on general policies for improving conditions for business development.

This was the point at which the Industry and Trade Development Council was formed. It has 22 members, who are, in principle, appointed by the Minister of Industry in their personal capacity but, in reality, on the basis of recommendations from the major organisations. According to interviewees, the Council is too large to be an effective forum for decision-making. The Industry and Trade Development Council Act states that the objectives of the Council are to support, contribute to, and evaluate with respect to:

- development and exploitation of technological, managerial, and market-based knowledge;
- R&D in the business enterprise sector;
- transformation of industry to meet the new challenges of society and competition;
- development of appropriate business infrastructure (capital formation, education, etc.);
- regulation in any area having an impact on business enterprises.

To fulfil its objectives, the Council had a budget of DKr 1 117 million in 1992. The amount included basic funding for technological service institutes, strategic programmes, support for development of individual companies, regional policy, tourism, and export promotion.

As regards co-ordination with the Danish Council for Research Policy, the Chairman of the Industry and Trade Development Council is one of 23 members of the representative body of the Danish Council for Research Policy (the Chairman of the Assembly of Chairmen for the National Research Councils is another).

Since its founding, the Council's two major tasks have been to restructure the system of technological service institutes, and perform eight major industry analyses based on a concept of "clusters of industries". Chapter VI deals in further detail with these tasks.

Structural changes

At this point it can only be concluded that a number of changes have been implemented in the high-level advisory structure since the 1987 OECD review of the Danish science and technology system. According to the interview results, these changes have not led to any better overall co-ordination of high-level policy by the advisory structure. On the contrary, the relations between the national research councils and the Danish Council for Research Policy are strained; indeed, the former are presently proposing the abolishment of the latter by the Minister of Research. Co-ordination is to all intents and purposes limited to the participation of one representative of the national research councils and one representative of the Industry and Trade Development Council in the 23-member representative body of the Danish Council for Research Policy.

Strengthening co-ordination between the Danish Council for Research Policy and the Industry and Trade Development Council (*e.g.* by a merger or by establishing joint committees for strategic planning) is apparently not even on the political agenda.

3. Evaluations

As indicated above, interviewees have generally been somewhat critical with respect to the lack of improvements in the overall co-ordination of STI policy both at the ministerial level and at the high advisory level. At the same time, they have generally been very positive about the major national evaluations performed since the late 1980s.

Denmark does not have a tradition of major evaluations, but owing to the 1987 OECD review of the Danish STI system and to the subsequent political pressure, a number of evaluations have been performed in the fields of physics, health, agriculture, energy, and environmental research. In general, these evaluations of research are viewed as a main instrument for ensuring that research activities are conducted in a coherent and effective way.

The national physics review was initiated at the request of the research community itself, which felt that the field, which had been a source of national pride, with outstanding scientists such as H.C. Ørsted and Niels Bohr, was now suffering from lack of funds for basic research and a general lack of scientific management. The physics review pointed to a number of structural adjustments to be made, among others a merging of the physics institutes at the University of Copenhagen into a single Niels Bohr Institute, with its own governing board and its own director. It also suggested a merger of some of the smaller physics institutes at the Technical University of Denmark and a better division of labour between the Technical University of Denmark and the University of Copenhagen. Most of these recommendations have been implemented, more or less as proposed, and prominent scientists in physics now express much confidence in the survival of an internationally-advanced scientific physics environment in Denmark.

The evaluation of Danish agricultural research was completed in 1992. It indicated that the quality and relevance of Danish agricultural research needed to be strengthened and that higher priority should be given to areas in which Denmark wished to excel at the international level. The Danish Council for Research Policy then recommended the development of a national strategy for state-funded agricultural research, one which would give higher priority to long-term strategic agricultural and environmental research. A committee which included the Advisory Committee for Agricultural Research (ACAR) was set up, and a national strategy in the field of agriculture was expected to be published in July 1994.

The national health evaluation led to fewer immediate structural improvements, but a national strategy is at present being developed in the field of health research. The national evaluation in environmental science and research led immediately to a number of structural adjustments, *e.g.* the merging of a number of institutes into the new Environmental Research Institute.

The national evaluations have affected the formulation and implementation of strategic programmes. Chapter IV gives further details on the strategic programmes, and Chapter V reviews some of the institutional mergers.

IV. STRATEGIC PROGRAMMES

The 1987 OECD review proposed a simplification of the intermediate policy level of the STI system, particularly with respect to the number of programmes, funding for strategic research, and bureaucracy, both for those applying for grants and for those operating schemes and programmes. Simplified procedures would also allow for better co-ordination across ministries and fields of science.

Since then, attempts have been made to establish R&D programmes that produce socially-relevant results and give "value for money". Better interaction between the different institutions and sectors of performance has been an important element as well. A rather large number of cross-ministerial and cross-sectoral strategic programmes have been implemented. Table IV.1 gives an overview of the major programmes in question, and the first section summarises the main characteristics of the various programmes.

This chapter deals with the evolution of the intermediate policy level since 1985, beginning with a chronological description of the major strategic programmes. A review of the major strategic programmes suggests that the STI system's ability to unite its forces by way of strategic programmes has improved considerably since 1987.

The chapter then discusses the extent to which strategic programmes have succeeded in stimulating STI activities that are more relevant for society, in establishing better interaction between institutions and sectors in the STI system, and in simplifying the intermediate policy level. Changes in the administration of the programmes have been an important element in the improvement of strategic programmes as a tool for influencing the STI system. Early programmes, such as the Action Plan for Research and Development (FTU), were criticised for insufficient co-operation between the research community and business enterprises, partly due to scarce administrative resources. A mid-period programme, such as the Food Technology Programme I (FØTEK I), suffered to some extent from the division of the administration among different ministries. However, most of the difficulties were eventually overcome by a co-ordination committee. The lessons learned from this experience led to the establishment of a joint administrative body for the Environmental Research Programme.

The chapter concludes that while improvements have been made, the overall problems still seem to be a lack of follow-through once a programme is terminated, programmes that are still too short despite recent attempts to lengthen them, and "stop and go" policies.

Table IV.1. **Overview of major R&D programmes**
(1987-93)

Programmes	Funding authorities	Administrative authorities	Period	Appropriations DKr millions
FTU – Action Plan for Research and Development	The Danish Research Councils: SNF, SSVF, SJVF, SSF, SHF, STVF	The Danish Research Councils: SNF, SSVF, SJVF, SSF, SHF, STVF	1985-90	293
TUP – The Danish Technological Development Programme	Ministry of Industry	The National Agency of Industry and Trade	1985-88	1 300
MUP I – The Danish Materials Technology Programme I	Ministry of Education and Research, Ministry of Industry, Research Councils: SNF and STVF	The former Danish Council of Technology Research, Councils: SNF, STVF and Co-ordination Committee	1988-92	495
MUP II – The Danish Materials Technology Programme II	Ministry of Education and Research, Ministry of Industry, Research Councils: SNF and STVF	Agency for Development of Trade and Industry, SNF, STVF and Co-ordination Committee	1994-97	414
BIOTEK I – The Danish Biotechnology Programme I	Ministry of Education and Research	Cross Departmental/Council Co-ordination Committee – appointed by the Government	1987-90	475
BIOTEK II – The Danish Biotechnology Programme II	Research Councils: SNF, STVF, SJVF, SSVF	Research Councils: SNF, STVF, SJVF, SSVF	1991-95	463
FØTEK I – The Danish Research and Development Programme for Food Technology I	Ministry of Industry, Ministry of Agriculture, Ministry of Research and Technology	Cross Departmental Co-ordination Committee	1990-94	545
FØTEK II – The Danish Research and Development Programme for Food Technology II	Ministry of Fisheries, Ministry of Research and Technology, Ministry of Agriculture, Ministry of Education, Ministry of Industry	Ministerial Grants Committees, Research Councils: SSVF, SJVF, SSF, STVF, Co-ordination Secretariat	1994-97	330
PIFT – The Danish Research Programme on Informatics	Research Councils: SNF, STVF, SJVF	Cross Council Co-ordination Committee	1991-94	212
Environmental Research – The Danish Environmental Research Programme	Ministry of Labour, Ministry of Energy, Ministry of Fisheries, Ministry of Research and Technology, Ministry of the Environment, Ministry of Agriculture, Ministry of Health, Ministry of Foreign Affairs	Management Group appointed by the Government	1992-96	300

Source: Monday Morning Strategic Forum, 1994.

1. Strategic programmes

This section deals with the main characteristics of major strategic R&D programmes since the mid-1980s. The programmes are reviewed in chronological order. Aside from these strategic programmes, a number of ministries – *e.g.* Agriculture, Environment, and Energy – are also important funders of R&D programmes; as an example, the funding activity of the Ministry of Energy is also reviewed.

The Technological Development Programme

The Technological Development Programme (TUP) was launched in 1985 and ended in 1988. Its source was a political debate in which the situation of Danish industry was compared to that of other industrialised countries, in which research and technology programmes focusing on new technologies were already being established. It was dedicated to the development of information technology in industry as a whole and received appropriations amounting to DKr 1.3 billion. The companies participating in the programme contributed an additional DKr 1.0 billion, and EU funding added DKr 0.2 billion. DKr 200 million was directed towards universities, institutions of higher education, and large scientific facilities that were at industry's disposal.

The Danish Council for Technological Development was in charge of the overall realisation of the programme, and the National Agency of Industry and Trade had administrative responsibility *via* project organisation.

When the TUP was evaluated, several positive conclusions were drawn:
- When the TUP was implemented, it was a relevant industrial development programme because it improved the business community's awareness of possibilities for applications of new technology. It also represented a new and effective way of developing and administering industrial policy.
- Although a detailed R&D programme of this sort had never previously been established and such programme organisation and administration had never been tried before, the programme had produced a useful basis for future efforts.
- The participating enterprises felt that the aim of improving their ability to adjust themselves to a higher technological level had, to a large extent, been reached. In addition, specific projects had in many cases strengthened the competitiveness of enterprises.
- The grantees considered that the programme had had significant impact on the technological infrastructure and the ability to create new knowledge and services for enterprises. However, enterprises used the new services only to a very limited extent.

There were also several criticisms:
- By placing the administration of the programme within an existing organisation, the potential extent of the programme was somewhat limited, and its detailed planning was limited by traditional practices.

- The political authorities terminated the programme a year earlier than originally planned, because they presumed that the programme had reached its goals. This action may have weakened industry's trust in the state as a contributor to the improvement of industrial competitiveness.
- Some enterprises used the appropriations for projects already started and thus in a sense as aid to enterprises with financial problems. It was not possible to ascertain to what extent such abuse had occurred, but it was not viewed as a serious problem.
- The programme caused enterprises to overestimate the possibilities of information technology.

Action Plan for Research and Development

At the same time as the TUP, the national research councils undertook a major initiative in order to meet the scientific and social challenges raised by the major technological developments of the mid-1980s by launching the Action Plan for Research and Development (FTU), the first major research programme administered jointly by the national research councils. It was funded and administered by the six national research councils. Its financial sources are listed in Table IV.2.

The national research councils evaluated the FTU twice, a mid-term evaluation in January 1988 and a final evaluation in 1991. The mid-term evaluation concluded that the FTU should not be continued as an isolated programme. Rather, the experience gathered from the programme should be used for future strategic research programmes. Further, it was important to maintain the economic base created during the programme for the research community.

The final evaluation of the FTU mainly assessed the administrative aspects of a programme of this length and scope. It also undertook a quantitative analysis of the transfer of results and of the experience gained by the research groups and researchers who had participated in FTU projects. Its main conclusions were that:

Table IV.2. **Financial sources of the FTU**

(DKr millions)

The Research Council of natural science	41.5
Technical science	169.8
Medical science	17.5
Agricultural and veterinary science	41.0
The humanities	7.7
Social sciences	14.2
Total	292.7

Source: Ministry of Education, 1991.

- Scarce administrative resources made it impossible to use planning groups with industry representatives to the extent originally planned.
- The programme was implemented during a period of high demand for scientists, which resulted in some difficulties in recruiting for programme projects. Nevertheless, more than 50 per cent of the approximately 100 participating scientists had completed their PhD training.
- It was a cause for concern that about 25 per cent of the projects did not imply any kind of collaboration between the research community and private enterprises.
- Overall, the FTU gave those responsible for administration and users the building blocks for future strategic research programmes.

The Materials Technology Development Programme

The original impetus for the first Materials Technology Development Programme (MUP I) was a proposal for a ten-year programme presented in 1987 by the former Council for Technological Development, the Technical Research Council, and the Natural Science Research Council. As eventually designed, the programme focused on technical and organisational recommendations made in this proposal, but within a five-year frame. Based on interest expressed by a broad range of figures in industry and research and subsequent hearings in the co-ordination committee, the programme was established.

Materials research plays a central role in Danish research. Industry's choice of materials increasingly depends on considerations of technological optimisation, the environment, and resources. Hence, the choice of appropriate materials is of increasing importance as a competitive factor. The programme focused on industry's development of new materials and materials processing.

MUP I was implemented over the period 1988-92. It received appropriations of DKr 495 million, with DKr 195 million from the budget of the Ministry of Education and Research, and DKr 300 million from that of the Ministry of Industry.

The Council for Technological Development, the Technical Research Council, and the Danish Natural Science Research Council had overall responsibility for the planning and administration of the programme. The planning was carried out in close co-operation with research institutes and members of the business community. The three councils shared administrative tasks through a co-ordination committee.

A mid-term evaluation focusing on five centres was presented in the spring of 1991. The evaluation committee concluded that:
- MUP made an important contribution to furthering the use of advanced, new, and improved materials.
- A national MUP should include strong efforts on basic materials science and on engineering: synthesis and processes, structure and composition, and properties and performance.
- The choice of areas to support and strengthen is difficult and must always be based on the needs of existing industries and on existing knowledge within

research institutes and other academic institutions. The choice of centres for the MUP followed the profile of corresponding programmes in other countries.
- The centres had a high level of industry participation, and they seemed to effectively bridge the gap between academic and industrial R&D.
- The five-year period allotted to the centres was far too short. It would take at least another two to three years for the R&D results from the best centres to be useful to Danish industry.
- A common education policy for the centres was lacking. Research activities should involve PhD and master's degree students.
- Participation in EU programmes was generally low. According to the centres, the reason was that the time spent on such collaboration did not give an adequate return. However, EU participation must be improved in future MUP projects.
- The committee recommended continuation at the same level of appropriations.

The evaluation clearly stated the need to continue the programme, and, as part of government initiatives to stimulate employment, MUP II will begin in 1994 and run through 1997. Its budget amounts to DKr 414 million. The Ministry of Research and the Ministry of Industry are responsible for carrying out the programme. The aims are to stimulate continued development of materials research at research institutions and in private enterprises and to ensure that Danish industry can exploit the results achieved so far.

The Biotechnological R&D Programme

The first Biotechnological R&D Programme (BIOTEK I) was established in 1987 by act of the Danish Parliament. It was active from 1987 to 1990 and received appropriations of DKr 475 million. It was financed by the Ministry of Education and Research and implemented by a cross-departmental/council committee and the Danish Research Administration.

The main aim of BIOTEK I was to encourage co-operation between universities and the biotechnology industry in order to accelerate industrial use of the results achieved and reinforce co-operation between universities and government research institutions. A further objective was to ensure an adequate supply of PhDs. Finally, it aimed to increase the international orientation of Danish biotechnological research.

A mid-term evaluation of BIOTEK I, performed in September/October 1989, concluded that:
- The co-ordination committee was too large, and this made it impossible to satisfy all the interests of all the ministries. The co-ordination improved cross-departmental contact but impeded the co-ordination of the relevant scientific areas. The committee should continue its work on the basis of a clearer cross-disciplinary profile.
- The "project culture" which characterised the centres conflicted with one of the main objectives of the programme: that funding, given as lump sum appropria-

tions, should not be focused on individual projects. The project culture makes the centres less flexible and adaptable.

- The establishment of centres has stimulated co-operation between university institutes, technological service institutes, government research institutions, and industry.
- That part of the programme relating to research training through the centres' recruitment of PhD students was a success. In the future, it is nonetheless essential that young researchers be able to do part of their research work abroad.
- Co-operative relations between institutions of higher education and industry have intensified, and both have developed a more positive attitude towards co-operation.

The evaluation concluded that, overall, the main result of BIOTEK I was a strengthening of co-operative research networks and of competence within these networks.

Priority areas for future biotechnological research were set on the basis of BIOTEK I. Its successor, BIOTEK II, runs from 1991 to 1995, with appropriations of DKr 463 million. It is a cross-council collaboration, and the national research councils for the natural sciences, medicine, agriculture, and technical sciences act as the funding and administrative authorities. The councils have established a cross-council co-ordination committee; there is also an advisory board with members from different ministries and organisations. A mid-term evaluation of the programme resulted in the following conclusions:

- The programme has greatly reinforced contacts and exchanges between the participating groups.
- The flexible funding structure of the programme has facilitated international relations, *e.g.* exchange of scientists; temporary recruitment of foreign specialists at appropriate times; and recruitment of PhD students and post-docs.
- The evaluation panel did not assess the weight of the funds provided by the programme relative to other sources of funding, because the panel had no knowledge of institutional funds, salaries, basic costs, etc. However, it acknowledged the importance and relevance of BIOTEK II funds.
- Given that the funds received by the centres decreased by 10 per cent a year, the panel expressed concern that the centres only were allowed to transfer 10 per cent of their annual BIOTEK allocation to the following year and recommended that 20 to 25 per cent be transferable.
- Some researchers appeared to be unaware of the rules of ethics and problems of liability, including those related to industrial property.
- The work and research results of the biotechnological centres were in many cases published in internationally-recognised journals.

The R&D Programme for Food Technology

The first R&D Programme for Food Technology (FØTEK I) was started in 1990 and runs through 1994 with state appropriations of DKr 545 million. It is carried out through interdepartmental co-operation between the Ministry of Industry, the Ministry of Agriculture (which contribute a total of DKr 375 million), and the Ministry of Research *via* four of the six national research councils (a grant of DKr 170 million). Industry is co-funding the programme with an additional DKr 300 million. A cross-departmental co-ordination committee is in charge of the overall management of the programme.

The programme's overall aim is to ensure that Denmark maintains and strengthens its competitive position in food technology on the international stage through the stimulation of industrial R&D.

In 1993, a scientific mid-term evaluation of the institutional part of the programme by an international panel resulted in the following conclusions:

- After a slow start, three research centres have been established at various institutions of higher education. As a result, collaboration between different research groups has been strengthened. The three centres are now placed under the National Food Centre.
- Collaboration between industry and the research community has increased. Of the DKr 355 million (government appropriations) spent so far, DKr 200 million were allocated to co-operative projects between private enterprises and research institutions (Ministry of Research and Technology, 1993). The three ministries involved in the programme have appropriated DKr 200 million, an amount matched by the participating business enterprises. An evaluation of FØTEK's direct effects on industry, in terms of the creation of new products, services, and marketing possibilities, is planned for 1994.
- Several of the projects are well directed, but a number of small projects lack guidance by senior scientists. The latter should be attached to larger and better-established groups.
- The number of PhD students is high, which will increase the availability of food scientists over the long term. However, the number of senior scientists is low, given the requirements of a large-scale programme such as FØTEK.

FØTEK has initiated many promising projects for the food industry, and it is very important that the programme continue in order to ensure that its original goals are reached. It is essential that future projects achieve an appropriate balance between industrial needs and scientific standards.

FØTEK II, launched in 1994, does not have a definite limit. It has appropriations of DKr 330 million for the period 1994-97. Like FØTEK I, FØTEK II is an interdepartmental programme, with co-operation by the ministries of Industry, Agriculture, Education, Fisheries, and Research.

The Research Programme on Informatics

The Research Programme on Informatics (PIFT) is a four-year research programme in information technology running from 1991 to 1994. It has received appropriations of DKr 212 million and is jointly funded by the Natural Science Research Council, the Technical Research Council, and the Agricultural and Veterinary Research Council. A co-ordination committee under the three research councils is in charge of the administration. The motivation for the programme is two-fold. First, Danish industry and business increasingly need research and education in the field of informatics, as well as co-operation among researches and users. Danish research groups also must be qualified to participate as equal partners in major EU research programmes in information technology.

An international panel appointed by the co-ordination committee of the research councils evaluated PIFT in June 1993 (mid-term evaluation). The evaluation furnished the basis for deciding on continuation of the programme. Its conclusions were:

- Originally, an industrial development programme was to be created in parallel with the informatics programme, but, because of a lack of political support, this was not done. PIFT has thus been characterised by an uneven balance between the focus on industrial needs and scientific aims.
- Interaction between industry and the research institutions was generally weak. According to some research centres, the reason was that industry was not yet ready for such advanced information technology.
- The standard of the research taking place in the research centres was often very high, although some projects did not fulfil expectations and others should probably have been transferred to industry.

The Environmental Research Programme

This programme, which is a co-ordinated programme involving eight ministries, was developed on a government initiative, after an international evaluation of Danish environmental research recommended a more focused funding procedure for environmental research on a long-term basis. The programme is endowed with DKr 300 million (DKr 60 million annually for programme activities) and runs from 1992 to 1996.

The programme's aim is to create frameworks for a stronger environmental research effort that will provide an improved knowledge base – strategic guidelines – for political and social decision-making process in this area. Research activities are directed towards gaining greater knowledge of the influence of human activity on the environment. They focus on harmful effects on the environment and the possible means to prevent or combat these effects. Finally, the programme must be, insofar as possible, related to international research programmes such as those of the EU. So far, eleven research centres without walls have been set up.

Energy research

Previous R&D efforts and a far-sighted energy policy have helped to ensure that Denmark is an international leader in certain fields of energy technology, such as district heating systems, wind energy, bio-fuels, flue gas cleaning systems, biomass combustion systems, etc.

Table IV.3. **Ministry of Energy R&D Programme
Distribution 1993**

(DKr millions)

Oil, gas	14.9
Biomass	6.5
Electricity, heating	19.9
Wind energy	8.8
Buildings, passive solar energy	11.4
Electricity saving	2.0
Fuel cells	9.1
Energy and society	8.2
International co-operation	8.0
Documentation	25.2
Strategic Environmental Programme	4.0
Technological development	15.0
Total	133.0

Source: Ministry of Energy, 1993.

The R&D programme of the Ministry of Energy plays an important role in sustaining Denmark's position. The distribution of funds for the programme is depicted in Table IV.3. The programme is supplemented by considerable private effort in the field as well as by subsidies for decentralised production of combined heat and power, for the exploitation of biofuel, and for the completion of the district heating network. Also, Nordic and EU R&D programmes in energy play an important role.

The programme was evaluated in 1993. The evaluation revealed that 50 per cent of the R&D funds are allocated to three institutions: the National Laboratory Risø, the Technical University of Denmark, and the Danish Technological Institute. Less than 5 per cent of the R&D funds were allocated to the business enterprise sector. According to a recent study on the energy and environment industry, this is a major problem for industry development.

2. Effects of the strategic R&D programmes

This section reviews and discusses the strategic programmes with respect to three main objectives: stimulating STI activities of social relevance and providing ''value for money'', strengthening interaction between the institutions and sectors of the STI system, and meeting the need to simplify the intermediate level.

STI activities relevant to society

One goal of the transformation of the Danish STI system is to encourage STI activities that meet social needs and have a useful effect, especially on industry. As suggested by the interviews at the performance and administrative level of the STI system, strategic programmes, especially the cross-council/ministerial programmes, have been an effective means of steering STI activities towards specific areas.

The first R&D programmes launched during the mid-1980s – the FTU and the TUP – differ a good deal from recent programmes such as FØTEK II and the Environmental Research Programme, whose objectives are far more well-defined and managed. This is obviously due to improved ability to define areas in need of R&D. The reason is, of course, that "learning by doing" strengthens the ability to establish programmes which clearly formulate the purpose of the programme and the "rules" by which those who apply for programme funds must abide. To reach the present state of things, many lessons have had to be learned.

The launching of the TUP and the FTU was the start of strategic programmes designed to stimulate and steer research, and, not surprisingly, the programmes suffered from the fact that objectives were very broadly defined and there were few possibilities of making a goal-directed effort. Yet the experience gained in those programmes was the foundation on which other R&D programmes could be established.

A specific weakness of early strategic programmes was insufficient interaction between academia and industry. This interaction is crucial if R&D programmes are to result in knowledge that is relevant for industrial innovation. In order to remedy this fault, cross-council and/or ministerial programmes such as FØTEK require industry to finance part of a research project. This is a way to "force" the research community and industry together and to ensure projects of industrial relevance.

By comparison to FØTEK I, FØTEK II is much more goal-directed. FØTEK I launched a broad range of projects relevant to industry, but it did not concentrate on a limited number of areas. It was therefore difficult to assess the quality and relevance of all the projects, and, as the mid-term evaluation of 1993 concluded, the quality of the research in the different projects varied a great deal. FØTEK II focuses on more research-intensive projects directed towards certain areas of research. This is an example of how lessons learned from one programme may improve subsequent programmes. Similarly, the research activities of BIOTEK II are more concentrated that those of BIOTEK I, *e.g.* activities related to foodstuffs are now under the auspices of FØTEK II.

According to interviewees, social relevance has also improved because the strategic programmes have introduced competition for funds. The applicants must now be open and aware of their strengths and weaknesses; they must prove their worth as grantees and cannot expect that they will automatically receive funding.

In general, both evaluations and interviews suggest that the strategic R&D programmes, as a tool for goal-directed research, have been successful, especially by creating more interaction between industry and the research community.

Interaction between institutions and sectors

As the STI system adapts itself to meeting social demands, the transformation of the system also has as a goal to create greater interaction and transfer of knowledge among institutions and sectors. As evaluations and interviews suggest, the cross-ministerial/council strategic programmes have often proved to be quite successful in stimulating interaction between institutions in the STI system, government research institutions, technological service institutes, universities and industry.

As previously noted, interaction between the research community and business enterprises is very important if R&D programmes are to reach a higher level of social relevance and "value for money". Years of experience have made the R&D programmes better at establishing a bridge between the different areas of the STI system.

In terms of the interaction between enterprises and the research community, interviews and programme evaluations generally concur that co-operation has improved. In general, R&D programmes increasingly create co-operative relations between industry and academia. The evaluations of FØTEK, BIOTEK II, and MUP conclude that these programmes have been able to establish contacts between industry and the public sector.

Nevertheless, relations between industry and academia can be improved. In many respects, researchers and industrialists have very different backgrounds and very different ways of thinking. Interviewees at the performance level pointed out that in order to establish a good relationship, the researcher must understand that the businessman has no interest in general long-term R&D projects whose concrete gains are unclear. The industrialist, instead, needs to understand that a researcher cannot deliver results ready for commercialisation immediately. In order to bridge the gap between academia and industry, people need to be prepared and to base their co-operation on mutual trust and understanding.

Another point made in the interviews was that strategic programmes are an efficient way to force different communities together, because that is where the money is. People are more inclined to co-operate and compromise when they know that there is no other way to obtain funds. In any case, co-operation between academia and industry is much more accepted now than in the 1970s, when each looked on the other with suspicion. Today, it is rather "in" for scientists to co-operate with industry.

The organisational framework for co-operation among institutions is either physical centres (as in the case of FØTEK), or so-called "centres without walls" (as in the case of BIOTEK and MUP I), in which project partners co-operate but work at different locations. The establishment of centres without walls has generally resulted in stronger interaction among institutions and has proved to be effective in combining knowledge and qualifications across institutions. Interviewees point both to their advantages and disadvantages. The primary advantage is that researchers exchange ideas and results on the basis of mutual interests and trust, and are not restricted by organisational boundaries. Also, researchers are able to maintain close contact with their home institutions, and not least with their students, whereas when they are located at a physical centre, they are isolated from their "community". Nevertheless, some interviewees emphasize that it is easier to manage and exploit competencies in physical centres, such as the Microelectronics Centre (at the Technical University), than in centres without walls. In general, centres without walls are not an unambiguous success.

Not all programmes have been able to establish co-operative links across sectors of performance and across institutions of the STI system. This is largely due to the fact that different interests, ways of thinking, and organisational boundaries work against greater interaction among the actors in the STI system. However, a process of learning by doing has improved cross-council/ministerial programmes, and programmes such as FØTEK II and the strategic Environmental Research Programme seem so far to have met the expectations of these recent strategic R&D initiatives.

Simplified administration and its effects

The 1987 OECD evaluation judged that the system of R&D programmes and funding for strategic research was bureaucratic and lacked transparency, both for those applying for grants and those operating schemes and programmes, and that this impeded the effectiveness of the strategic programmes.

Since then, owing to the rather large number of cross-ministry and/or cross-council strategic programmes, the amount of administrative work has increased and the administration has had difficulty in managing the increase. According to interviews and programme evaluations, the administration of FØTEK I was very inefficient and bureaucratic, and consequently the programme had a slow start. The experience of the 1980s and 1990s has resulted in improved strategic programmes and new programme models. Those interviewed saw the small and efficient independent management of the Environmental Research Programme as a good way to avoid many of the administrative problems. However, such *ad hoc* groups are less suited to assuring the continuity of activities after a programme is terminated.

Users have three main criticisms of the administration of the strategic programmes. First, the work connected with applications, progress reports, evaluations, etc., takes a vast amount of time and resources. Some of the interviewees said that all the administrative work left no time to do research, but there was no consensus on an overall solution. One respondent had solved the problem of "administrative overload" by hiring a person with experience in national and international R&D programmes who was placed in charge of programme applications, reports, etc., thus shifting the burden of paperwork away from the researchers and their activities.

Second, the administrative and funding authorities of cross-council/ministerial programmes often have completely different administrative procedures; this complicates the management of projects and centres and makes the system somewhat unclear for users. Users sometimes find it difficult to see the purpose of all the reports and evaluations, and the objective of the programme may be blurred by controversies between the granting authorities. Again, FØTEK has obviously suffered from disagreements and controversies between the ministries involved.

Third, users often criticise the lack of specific expertise among funding and administrative authorities, who do not have the necessary insight into the research fields and sometimes distribute funds in a random manner without considering the quality of applicants' work. In general, they find the intermediate administrative level impenetrable and do not see what criteria programme authorities use to select grantees and evaluate projects. A clearer structure would improve the credibility of the programme administrators. Here again, the Environmental Research Programme has a structure and management that is clear and well-arranged. The criteria and "rules" are clear, and grantees feel that they are professionally and fairly treated.

Disagreements and differences among programme authorities may result in sudden alterations in the funding criteria, and this directly affects the grantees. However, some alterations and adjustments have been due to attempts to strengthen the strategic R&D programmes. The burdensome administration of BIOTEK II was due to the fact that the programme authorities had to "clean up" after BIOTEK I. In comparison to FØTEK I, FØTEK II has also become more centralised and has placed the three FØTEK centres under the National Food Centre. In FØTEK I the obligation to co-operate with industry was couched in economic terms, whereas in FØTEK II it is specified in scientific and technological terms. This ensures greater flexibility in the performance of the National Food Centre and other participating institutes.

For those administering the cross-ministerial/council programmes (members of co-ordination committees, etc.) the main point of criticism is the number of interests to be considered. This is very time-consuming, delays the work, and makes it difficult to ensure the necessary level of flexibility. When different ministries and councils participate directly in the administration of a programme, the challenge is often to create a common set of goals and mutual interests. This challenge is difficult, because ministries and councils naturally have different objectives, and especially their administrative procedures can be very different. Hence, a cross-ministerial/council programme must be based on a clearly-formulated set of "rules and objectives" understood by and agreed to by all parties. This implies that strategic programmes involving several authorities have to be carefully prepared before they are launched.

The Environmental Research Programme went through a long period of preparation during which all the participating ministries presented their objectives. After long discussions – some say too long – the ministries finally agreed upon common terms of reference and subsequently gave the programme management group a mandate to distribute the appropriations allocated by each ministry. Once they had approved the programme, the ministries abstained from intervention in the management of the programme.

FOTEK II offers a second example of an attempt to avoid administrative problems. Joint financing of the programme activities by the ministries has been replaced by funding by each of the participating ministries. This greatly reduces the administrative problems that characterised FØTEK I.

Programme committee members feel that the (unsalaried) work they perform in co-ordination committees, steering groups, etc., is time-consuming and encroaches on their leisure time, and they call for some kind of compensation. This may mean that less-qualified work is performed and that programme committee members are replaced too frequently, a situation which does not ensure the necessary continuity and experience among programme authorities. However, interviewees suggested no specific solutions.

Those on the administrative side point out that problems often arise when too many parties participate in the direct management of the programme. The fewer, the better.

The consequence of the weaknesses in the management of R&D programmes mentioned above is that programmes are terminated without appropriate follow-up that would ensure optimal exploitation of results.

V. PUBLIC SECTOR R&D

This chapter begins by reviewing the OECD 1987 recommendations and their impact on the structure and activities of public sector STI and then discusses the main actors at the performing level. Next, the initiatives taken by some institutions to reorganise their management in order to improve their ability to govern themselves are described. It is concluded that it is important to sustain and broaden the trend towards institutional self-governance, and that the issue is "how" rather than "if". Measures such as the recruitment of external, professional managers and long-term agreements between the government and individual institutions, using agreed evaluation criteria, are discussed, along with some inherent structural problems, such as the composition of public sector STI staff with respect to age and sex, are identified and discussed as well. Finally, the new National Research Foundation and recent initiatives by the Danish Research Academy are presented.

With respect to public sector R&D, the 1987 OECD review made the following proposals:

- Activities within existing institutions should be consolidated and developed rather than establishing new institutions to meet changing needs and priorities.
- University autonomy should be increased, and the organisational and administrative system should be simplified and strengthened.
- Measures should be taken to lower the high drop-out rate and produce more scientifically- and technically-trained graduates.
- Mechanisms to stimulate students with a lower-level technical degree to continue their studies towards the MSc and PhD should be reinforced.
- Institutions of higher education should continue to receive block grant funds for basic uncommitted research, and funding for strategic research should be simplified.

Since 1987 many new activities have been developed within existing institutions. The concept of "centres without walls" has been implemented as a tool for meeting new strategic challenges in most cases where specific needs and priorities have been identified.

The new University Act has increased university autonomy. Measures aimed at a general lowering of drop-outs in institutions of higher education and other measures for improving the production of PhDs have also been implemented.

Higher education institutions continue to receive block grant funds for basic research, but in general, the number of sources of external funding has increased since 1987, as has the share of external funding in total funding of research at higher education institutions.

1. Main performers of R&D

The main public-sector performers of R&D are institutions of higher education, government research institutes, and private non-profit R&D institutions.

Institutions of higher education

R&D performers in institutions of higher education are found in general universities as well as in specialised ones (*e.g.* architecture, the Royal Academy of Arts). Table V.1 indicates the major players along with their total 1991 R&D expenditure. The 14 institutions listed account for 98 per cent of total R&D expenditure in the higher education sector.

In order to concentrate national R&D resources, institutes and institutions have merged in two areas. First, the two universities specialised in odontology have been merged with the general universities of Copenhagen and Aarhus. Second, a major restructuring of the Royal Veterinary and Agricultural University has reduced the number of institutes from 40 to 13.

Table V.1. **Institutions of higher education**
Major R&D performers 1991
Total R&D expenditure

(DKr millions)

University of Copenhagen	878
The Technical University of Denmark	597
University of Aarhus	562
The Royal Veterinary and Agricultural University	253
University of Aalborg	212
University of Odense	200
Copenhagen Business School	103
University of Roskilde	93
Danish Pharmacological University	77
Aarhus Business School	37
The School of Dentistry, Copenhagen	35
Royal Academy of Arts	35
The School of Dentistry, Aarhus	29

Source: Ministry of Research and Technology, *Forskning og udviklingsarbejde i den offentlige sektor 1991*, Copenhagen 1992.

74

Some policy co-ordination is ensured by the Danish Rectors' Conference, established as a co-operative body by the rectors of the institutions of higher education and universities in 1967, which presently has representatives from 18 different institutions of higher education and a secretariat that manages routine activities. The Conference also participates in various international bodies such as the Liaison Committee of the Rectors' Conference of Member States of the European Community and the CRE (Standing Conference of rectors, presidents and vice-chancellors of European universities).

Government research institutes

According to national research statistics (*Forskning og Udviklingsarbejde i den offentlige sektor*, Ministry of Research and Technology, Copenhagen, 1992, Annex) government research institutes can be subdivided into:

- hospitals and primary health care, with 110 institutions, including the Government Serum Institute as well as the Danish Hospital Institute (however, university hospitals fall under higher education);
- museums, libraries, and archives, with 68 institutions;
- agricultural research institutions, with 44 institutions;
- government research establishments, with 47 institutions, among them the Risø National Laboratory, the Government Serum Institute, and the State Veterinary Laboratory.

The government research institutes are obviously very different, but within the limits of this report, it is not possible to describe the differences in detail. Table V.2 lists the major government research institutes, along with their total 1991 R&D expenditure. The 23 institutions listed cover 73 per cent of total government research institute R&D in 1991.

In terms of restructuring, a separate dairy research unit (*Statens Mejeriforsøg*) was abandoned in 1990, and its tasks were divided among the business sector, which took up a large part of the responsibility for applied and strategic R&D, and the Royal Danish Veterinary and Agricultural University, which took up major responsibility for basic R&D.

In 1991, R&D related to agricultural construction and building was concentrated by transferring certain departments from the Danish Building Research Institute to the National Institute of Agricultural Engineering.

Similarly, R&D in the area of fisheries was concentrated by the formation of the Danish Institute for Fisheries, Technology, and Aquaculture, which incorporates a number of formerly distinct government research institutes. A new research administration has been set up in the Ministry of Fisheries, and a separate advisory board on R&D in the area has been created.

Some policy co-ordination at the performing level is ensured by the Assembly of Directors of Government Research Establishments, to which the various government research establishments appoint a representative. Its functions are to act as a forum for debate and information, to formulate guidelines for a common policy on research policy

Table V.2. **Government research institutions**
Major R&D performers 1991
Total R&D expenditure
(DKr millions)

Rigshospitalet (Government Hospital)	256
Government Serum Institute	76
Odense Municipal Hospital	56
Aarhus Municipal Hospital	40
Hvidovre Municipal Hospital	39
Copenhagen Municipal Hospital, Herlev	53
Skejby Municipal Hospital	36
Copenhagen Municipal Hospital, Gentofte	38
Aarhus Psychiatric Hospital	23
Aarhus County Hospital	24
The National Museum	46
State Veterinary Laboratory	210
The National Institute of Animal Science	124
Risø National Laboratory	350
Danish Environmental Research Institute	108
Geological Survey of Denmark	66
Danish Building Research Institute	63
National Institute of Social Research	31
National Food Agency of Denmark	45
Danish Defense Research Establishment	40
National Institute of Occupational Health Denmark	25
Geological Survey of Greenland	36
Danish Space Research Institute	25

Source: Ministry of Research and Technology, *Forskning og udvikling i den offentlige sektor 1991*, Copenhagen 1992.

matters, to increase the visibility of government research establishments, and to strengthen the representation of government research in discipline-specific councils and committees.

Private non-profit R&D institutions

Private non-profit R&D institutions form a third sub-group of public sector R&D. Of the 24 institutions belonging to this group, the most important is the Cancer Foundation, which spent DKr 82 million on R&D in 1991 and accounted for 49 per cent of total private non-profit R&D.

2. Funding of public sector R&D

Public sector R&D is funded largely from institutional (or ''core'') funding, which accounts, on average, for 68 per cent of public sector R&D funding; the share varies little

Table V.3.   **Public sector expenditures on R&D by sector of performance, source of finance**

(percentage of total, 1991)

	Higher education	Government research institutions	Private non-profit R&D institutes	Total
Own funds/basic funding	68	66	75	68
Research councils	9	3	2	6
Other public funding	12	14	4	13
Business enterprises	2	4	4	3
Organisations/private funds	5	9	7	6
EU-schemes and programmes	2	2	1	2
Other foreign sources	2	2	7	2
Total	100	100	100	100

Source: Ministry of Research and Technology, *Forskning og udviklingsarbejde i den offentlige sektor 1991*, Copenhagen 1992.

across sub-sectors. As Table V.3 indicates, other public funding is the second most important source of funding for both institutions of higher education and government research institutes. The National Research Councils also play an important role both for institutions of higher education and government research institutes.

External funding has increased constantly since 1981 (Table V.4). Both institutions of higher education and government research institutes now finance one-third of their R&D from external funding. In 1981, institutions of higher education funded 14 per cent of R&D through external funding and government research institutes, 17 per cent.

Interviewees both in universities and in government research question the present balance of basic and external funding. In government research, it is generally felt that basic appropriations are now so low that it is very difficult to maintain the production of basic knowledge. External funders often assume that institutes contribute some of their basic appropriations to externally-funded projects. In fact, the tables underestimate the actual amount of externally-funded activities. Further, government research institutes often have administrative tasks to fulfil in addition to their research tasks, and their basic appropriations are meant to cover these costs as well. This reduces the resources available for maintaining the scientific knowledge base.

Government research institutes have signalled their willingness to play an important role in the STI system. In a statement of the Board of Directors for Government Research Establishments (December 1993) and an agreement of April 1994 between the agricultural sector and the government, government research institutes define an important strategic role for themselves in producing scientific research oriented towards the needs and goals of society. By contrast, the role of universities is to perform basic research to meet purely scientific goals and that of technological service institutes is to conduct market-oriented research and to act as consultants.

Table V.4. **Public sector expenditures on R&D by sector of performance and source of finance**

Own sources/basic funds and external funds

(percentage of total, 1981-91)

	1981	1983	1985	1987	1989	1991
Higher education						
Own sources/basic funds	86	84	81	76	71	68
External funds	14	16	19	24	29	32
Government research institutions						
Own sources/basic funds	83	81	79	75	71	67
External funds	17	19	21	25	29	33
Private non-profit R&D institutions						
Own sources/basic funds	80	82	85	81	78	76
External funds	20	18	15	19	22	24
Total						
Own sources/basic funds	84	83	80	76	71	68
External funds	16	17	20	24	29	32

Source: Ministry of Research and Technology, *Forskning og udviklingsarbejde i den offentlige sektor 1991*, Copenhagen 1992.

Some government research institutes interviewed indicate that they deliberately refrain from market-oriented research and consulting because undertaking these activities would affect what they see as the division of labour with technological service institutes. At the same time, they feel that they possess scientific capabilities which could be usefully exploited, notably by the business enterprise sector. Also market-oriented research tasks and consulting offer government research institutes tempting ways to compensate for decreasing basic appropriations and maintain their previous level of STI activities.

Universities, and individual scientists or groups of scientists at universities, offer government research institutes strong competition for the production of scientific research oriented towards the needs and goals of society, areas which are receiving increasing amounts of STI funds. This changing orientation is successful in the sense that STI activities are in fact more directed towards meeting these needs and goals. At the same time, however, it disturbs the division of labour between universities, government research institutes, and possibly technological service institutes.

From the perspective of government research institutes, universities compete unfairly, often using their basic appropriations to supplement external funds, and thereby augmenting the amount of research they do under grants for societal research. As a number of government research institutes put it, ''Universities do not stick to their job as performers of basic research.'' In fact, a number of interviewees argue that, by competing for grants for societal research, universities neglect basic research to such an extent that the quality of basic research in some fields is now unacceptably low. Finally, government research institutes point out that fair competition, which they welcome, would be possible if overhead expenditures were calculated differently when granting money for this kind of research.

The universities also see increased external funding of STI activities as a threat to basic research, first of all because of the time they spend applying for funds, given that they apply to a variety of funds and programmes, each with different procedures and rules. The time and resources spent on applying for external funds are taken from the basic appropriations, which are intended for basic research.

Universities interviewed do not see problems of competition and division of labour *vis-à-vis* government research institutes and technological service institutes. Universities have been urged to engage in more research oriented towards the needs and goals of society. They do see as a major problem the increased number of students to be educated, since the relevant resources do not cover actual costs. The increase in the number of candidates, noted in Chapter I as a major feature of the social change in the 1980s, in reality then is made at the expense of the effort in basic research.

3. Strengthening basic research and PhD production

Since the mid-1980s and in parallel with the trend towards increased external funding of public sector STI, attempts have been made to stimulate basic research and production of PhDs. A National Research Academy and a National Research Foundation have been founded to this end, and there has been a new PhD reform. The national research councils also play an important role in funding basic research activities.

The National Research Foundation

The Danish National Research Foundation was established in 1991 following discussions on ways to improve basic research and create centres of excellence at the international level. While the Max Planck institutes were a source of inspiration, it was agreed that, in Denmark, basic research and higher education should be closely linked. The argument for a new institution, rather than allocation of funds by the national research councils, was that National Research Foundation grants should exceed by an order of magnitude what national research councils normally allocate. The Foundation is an autonomous institution, under the supervision of the Ministry of Research.

The Foundation's main objective is to finance unique Danish research at the international level; its funding represents 2.5 per cent of the overall annual public research budget. Moreover, it aims to enhance the development of Danish research by providing the best scientists with favourable opportunities for development, by increasing internationalisation, and by contributing to improved education of researchers.

Foundation grants are largely given as substantial and flexible grants to be used at the discretion of the recipients and for a period of three to five years. Nevertheless, to receive the annual payments, recipients must carry out the approved plans at an appropriate professional level. Continuation beyond the initial period is contingent on evaluation by internationally-recognised scientists.

The grants are awarded for an approved research activity and are based on a principle of total funding, *i.e.* they cover salaries as well as equipment and operating costs. Unlike many co-financed activities, the activities funded by the Foundation must not be supplemented by grants from other sources, except when the purpose is to expand the activities and/or establish international co-operation. Interviews at the performing level indicate, however, that the grants do not cover all costs.

The criteria for awarding grants include the likelihood that the research will have international impact, its relevance for Denmark, the prospects of co-operation with universities and other institutes of advanced education, and possibilities for co-operation with scientists from other countries.

In order to assess the needs, problem areas, and research plans of the various actors in the STI system, the Foundation works closely with the national research councils, the universities and institutions of higher education, government research institutes, technological service institutes and private enterprises. It draws on the research councils for professional scientific evaluation of proposals.

In May 1992, the Foundation issued a call for proposals and received 350. It has chosen to support 23 research centers and research groups for the next five years. The groups and centres cover almost all research disciplines and are located at existing universities and research institutions. The aim is to create within five years research groups and centres which are among the best in Europe or on a global scale.

The Research Academy

Established in 1986, the Danish Research Academy is responsible for stimulating and co-ordinating postgraduate study in Danish universities and academic colleges. At its foundation, the Academy's immediate objective was to increase the training of researchers in Denmark in terms of both quantity and quality. Its overall goal was to increase the number of internationally competitive "trained brains" at the doctoral level.

The Academy has the following functions:
- It acts as an advisory body to the Ministry of Education on matters concerning postgraduate training and the implementation of the PhD reform, including the distribution of scholarships among institutions of higher education.
- It stimulates co-operation by institutions of higher education, government research establishments, and enterprises that perform R&D.
- It provides studentships for postgraduate studies for students who wish to take a full PhD degree abroad (three years).
- It is a focal point for Danish participation in international initiatives concerning research education.

Table V.5. Grants distributed among programmes, 1993

(DKr millions)

	Basic appropriations	External funds	Research Academy total
Studies abroad	17.0	–	17.0
Guest professors	4.0	–	4.0
Guest scholars	2.0	–	2.0
Research education courses/summer schools/networks	7.0	1.0	8.0
Scholarship programmes	30.0	–	30.0
Co-financed scholarships	25.0	50.0	75.0
Nordic scholarships	1.0	0.5	1.5
DANVIS	6.0	–	6.0
Total	92.0	51.5	143.5

Source: Danish Research Academy, 1993.

The Academy's budget for 1993 is presented in Table V.5. Its main programmes are the Stimulation Programme, the Fellowship Programme, the Interface Programme and the DANVIS Programme, which is described in Chapter VIII.

The Stimulation Programme, one of the first programmes implemented by the Academy, was aimed at strengthening the internationalisation, mobility, and quality of Danish doctoral programmes by awarding grants for studies abroad and by inviting guest professors and scholars to participate in Danish doctoral programmes.

The Fellowship Programme was established in 1988 and focuses on stimulating industry and public sector co-financing of scholarships in order to improve the quality of R&D in these sectors. The scholarship grants have three parts: one-third goes to the institution, one-third to the project, and one-third covers expenditures by the co-operative partners. The target is to create at least 300 fellowships, and between 1991 and 1993, 257 agreements were made.

The Interface Programme was the Academy's first scholarship programme. Its goal was to attract more students to doctoral programmes directly from the undergraduate level.

The reform of the PhD

On 1 January 1993 a reform of postgraduate studies leading to the PhD degree took effect. Its aim is, first, to strengthen the quality of the content and supervision of the PhD programme. Second, it seeks to harmonize national standards for doctoral study with international standards. Finally, it makes available a new type of studentship, in order to attract more and younger students to postgraduate study. The reform has four elements:

– an addition to the State Grant Scheme Act (10 July 1992);
– a Ministerial Order concerning the PhD degree (11 December 1992);
– a budget of approximately DKr 100 000 per year per enrolled student to cover expenses incurred by institutions of higher education in connection with the PhD programme;
– an agreement between the Ministry of Finance and the Danish Confederation of Professional Associations on pay for PhD students.

Research students have hitherto been responsible for covering their own living expenses during their studies and the writing of their theses, whereas students enrolled for bachelor's or master's degrees have been, and still are, entitled to state grants (under the State Grant Scheme). Research students have had access to funding from:

– work-related project grants facilitated by the Academy of Technical Sciences and financed by the Danish Agency for Development of Trade and Industry/the Ministry of Industry;
– institutions of higher education which have had at their disposal a number of grants comparable to the negotiated state salary in the category (about DKr 250 000);
– grants from the Academy of Technical Sciences, partly the Academy's own grants, partly co-financing with governmental research institutes, corporations, etc.;
– grants from the research councils;
– salaried positions with a research institute or a company while working for their degree.

In addition, the State Grant Scheme does not entitle PhD students to grants at the same level as those for bachelor's and master's degrees. The individual research student is still responsible for finding funding through the existing sources; however, individual students should not be so dependent on salaried work on the labour market.

Postgraduate studies are now viewed as an integral part of the educational system. With the reallocation of funding, the State Grant Scheme can cover expenses incurred by institutions in mounting the now obligatory study programmes that precede the degree, which include supervision, courses and seminars, travel and study abroad, etc. The Ministerial Order concerning the PhD degree has meant intensified requirements for the PhD degree, which was previously awarded on the basis of the thesis alone. Mandatory registration for a three-year period at the relevant institution is now also a condition for obtaining the PhD.

In the past, standards for the PhD were set with respect to Danish national standards alone. They implied a level of achievement between the master's degree (awarded after a five-year university course of study) and the doctor's degree (a senior degree awarded for a major contribution to research). The Danish PhD degree is now correlated with international standards for PhD studies, *i.e.* those of the United Kingdom and the United States, where the PhD degree programme includes taught courses, seminars, etc., as well as the thesis. Apart from facilitating the acceptance of Danish PhD students abroad, the main aim of the new order is to maintain a high level of quality, despite the expressed intention of increasing the number of PhD students considerably, and to have a course of study that is completed within a few years of the master's degree.

Under the new scheme, the PhD programme will correspond to three years of study, and students must have completed a master's degree before entering it. During the PhD programme, research students will follow courses corresponding to approximately six months of work, participate in two or more active research groups or networks, preferably abroad, gain experience in the communication of knowledge, and carry out an independent research project resulting in a thesis.

The agreement between the Danish Confederation of Professional Associations and the Ministry of Finance stipulates a wage for work carried out by PhD students. Students receiving the PhD studentship under the State Grant Scheme are also offered salaried employment corresponding to 840 hours of work and amounting to about DKr 159 000.

The implementation of one of the main elements of the reform – the structured study programme – requires the relevant institutions to build adequate programmes. This means extra costs for the institutions in question, which are calculated to be some DKr 100 000 per year per enrolled student. They will generally be covered through the allocation of resources matched to PhD studentships from the State Grant Scheme, and institutions that have been given a number of studentships will also be entitled to a "fare" subsidy for each student to cover the various basic costs. However, if an institution does not obtain grants from the State Scheme or wishes to award more studentships than it has been allocated from the State Scheme, these costs may be covered by other sources.

Institutions can enrol students on the basis of other criteria than the ones used for the "fare" subsidies, as long as they carry the expenses themselves. If an institution enrols students who are funded by external sources, such as the research councils or research institutes, the latter will normally be expected to pay a sum corresponding to the "fare" subsidy.

4. Steps towards institutional self-governance in the university sector

The main development in public sector R&D since the mid-1980s has been the increased external funding of both universities and government research institutes. At the same time, other changes have strengthened institutional self-governance, notably in institutions of higher education, owing to the new University Act.

Under the former administrative framework, apart from the Rector's competence to act in special cases, universities had no well-defined internal or external decision-making responsibility. Consequently, they were rather weak co-operative partners and, in light of the internal and external changes which had taken place during the 1980s, seemed somewhat out-of-date. Due to their managerial weaknesses, universities lacked the ability to plan and lead research activities. Furthermore, no one was responsible for the planning and quality of teaching.

The new University Act intends to strengthen university management and interviewees indicate that, although the Act is very recent, a number of initiatives indicate that institutions intend to take advantage of the new possibilities it offers.

Government research institutes have not been motivated to strengthen their managerial capabilities in the same way, but they are taking the same kind of initiatives as universities in order to strengthen their managerial capabilities. According to interviewees, in fact, government research institutes have generally gone even further than universities in this respect.

The rest of this section is devoted to a discussion of the University Act and the so-called multi-annual agreement. Finally, some managerial initiatives are described and remaining barriers for the effective management of both universities and government research institutes are discussed.

The University Act

First and foremost, the Act is based on the principle of self-governance, in terms of the use of economic resources and the planning and content of studies. The reason for previous managerial problems lies in the legislative framework of the previous Administration Act (1973), which made the so-called "two-string" system. This two line of authority system was the basis of the self-governance structure of universities. In this system, student-staff committees were placed under a central student-staff committee, which had no connection with the remaining structure, so that decisions taken in student-staff committees could not be submitted either to faculty councils or to the Academic Council. Moreover, under that system, appropriations and the planning of teaching were placed in different units. Under the new governance structure, student-staff committees are placed under the faculty councils, and the responsibility for appropriations and teaching have been placed in the same organisational unit.

Under the new structure, whose main purpose is to ensure co-ordination and coherence among the various decision-making levels, the rector heads the entire university and has formal responsibility for the management of staff. The managerial hierarchy is as follows:

- The top level includes the rector and the Academic Council. They are in charge of the planning and implementation of the overall guidelines of the institution and approve proposals for the budget and statutes.
- The second level includes, on the one hand, the faculty councils in charge of the planning and formulation of the overall guidelines of the institutes/departments and approval of budgets and *syllabi* and, on the other, the deans who are charged with routine activities.
- The third level includes the governing bodies of departments/institutes, which establish general guidelines for the institute and approve the budget within the framework stipulated by the faculty councils, as well as the heads of department, who have responsibility for planning department/institute guidelines and approving budgets.

At this third level, the student-staff committees, each consisting of an equal number of teachers and students, approve *curricula* and present suggestions for study programmes. Finally, on behalf of the rector, the study programme director manages the practical planning of studies, disposes of the resources allocated to them, and is responsible for the content of study programmes.

One objective of the new Act is to ensure a certain level of quality and efficiency, for example by strengthening the role of external examiners. The new legislative framework also implies greater emphasis on evaluations of study programmes. Quality and efficiency are assessed thanks to a clear definition and distribution of responsibility. Student influence on the planning and quality of studies is ensured partly through their representation in student-staff committees, partly through their right to direct complaints to the study programme director.

The head of department has the day-to-day responsibility for departmental studies and is in charge of the use of the available resources. He/she also organises and implements research activities and formulates the research profile of his/her institute/department, for example by establishing research groups to carry out research activities on the basis of the plans and objectives of the institute/department in question.

The new legislative framework simplifies the administrative structure of the universities both internally and with respect to external bodies. The number of governing bodies in universities has been reduced, and each can have at most 15 members, half the number under the former framework. This rationalisation of the governance structure makes more resources available for other purposes, primarily research and teaching activities.

While it is too early to evaluate the impact of the Act, there are indications that managerial capabilities have improved and that universities are using them as intended.

In the mid-1980s, one major university introduced the practice of conducting internal professional evaluations of research at the department level every third year. While this initially led to some conflicts between different types of science, *e.g.* natural sciences and social sciences, researchers gradually became accustomed to these evaluations and began to act in accordance with the evaluation criteria in order to obtain as good an evaluation as possible. These evaluations were also used for allocating basic research funds among departments, and departments that received below average evaluations could not hire new researchers when positions became available. To some extent, this made positions for researchers available to departments with higher ratings. The University Act will probably allow the university in question to extend the use of evaluations as a management tool. Evaluation by external professionals and the introduction of "market analysis" and studies of present or potential competitive positions are possible next steps.

University management foresees a move towards national specialisation of universities and increased international competition with other universities with similar profiles. By 1996, the Nordic countries will create an internal market for university education that will radically increase competition among them. The main competitive parameter will be an outstanding research profile, and the university referred to above, as well as others interviewed, seem to be aware of, and preparing for, this situation.

The same university manages research both by top-down measures, such as resource allocation on the basis of evaluations, and by bottom-up procedures. Top-down management has allowed the university to create a pool of "free resources" that is being used for its strategic research. Research projects that meet the university's strategic research goals are funded from basic appropriations not allocated to departments and are selected through "bottom-up" procedures.

Another major university has recently introduced a similar research management process, at the faculty, rather than the university, level. It also foresees national specialisation in research (and accordingly in higher education) among universities and increased competition for students among Nordic countries.

The multi-annual agreement

In 1992, the Parliament adopted the so-called "multi-annual agreement", which covers the period 1993-96 and provides a basis for long-term planning for university research. By the terms of the agreement, universities and other institutions of higher education receive an overall block grant. They then determine their own priorities and distribute the appropriations to major areas and purposes – teaching, research, etc. Productivity savings related to the basic appropriations for research are then channelled back to the institutions from which they were taken. It is the role of institutional management to decide which areas to strengthen.

In order to improve productivity and reduce drop-outs, teaching is now financed by the so-called "fare" concept, by which a certain amount of money is assigned to each student who completes a year of study. Given that the government only pays for students who actually complete an academic year, the institutions are very concerned about reducing drop-outs. The principle also encourages institutions to ensure that students do not take longer than absolutely necessary to finish their studies. At present, the amount paid per student per year is announced annually, but the government intends to secure a multi-annual agreement on the fare amounts.

A bibliometric seminar held in Copenhagen in January 1994 indicated that such an effort developing appropriate tools and measures should probably be organised on an Scandinavian or a Nordic basis and possibly in the form of an "Observatory for Science and Technology" as known from a French, and now Dutch, setting. A permanent institution such as an Observatory for Science and Technology could fulfil other tasks requested during interviews and during a round-table discussion held in Copenhagen in April 1994. During the round-table discussion a need was raised and discussed for a permanent research evaluation institution assisting individual institutions in regular self-evaluations as well as councils etc. in performing evaluations in specific fields of science, the impact of specific programmes etc. combining self-evaluations with external evaluations. Chapter VI discusses the need for such an Observatory for Science and Technology from a technology assessment and forecasting point of view.

Government study grants for students have also changed. Each student who has a right to a study grant (depending on own or parents' level of income) can obtain the grant only for the number of years corresponding to the estimated time of study (bachelor's degree, three years, and master's degree, two years, for a total of five years). Beyond that, no study grants are available.

Interviewees indicate that the multi-annual agreement and the "fare" concept have markedly facilitated the move towards institutional self-governance. At both the performing and administrative level, they suggest the possibility of taking the approach further. They note that basic appropriations appear to be distributed very conservatively among universities and are not very dependent on evaluations of total university research performance. In due time, the introduction of evaluation criteria for the allocation of basic appropriations for research among universities might also be considered. At most universities, basic appropriations for research constitute 40 to 50 per cent of total institutional turn-over; at some universities, the share is less but still around one-third of the total budget.

Especially if basic appropriations for research are increased, it seems clear that allocations among universities should be based on strategic planning and evaluation criteria. In such a case, new analytical tools, such as sophisticated bibliometric methods combined with more qualitative measures, need to be developed.

Government research institutes

Government research institutes have not received the same political attention regarding managerial conditions and capabilities as have universities. Nevertheless, according to interviewees, strategic planning and research management have been widely introduced.

One government research establishment has been using bibliometric indicators very rigorously for five years for the allocation of appropriations for research among departments and researchers. Research evaluations have not been published externally, but all researchers and departments have received their individual rankings in the establishment in question.

Another government research institute has performed major strategic analysis of its own strengths and weaknesses, in the European, Nordic, and national context, and on that basis has established its strategic profile.

Elsewhere, there has been less strengthening of strategic planning and research management, but attitudes and procedures have changed in the very recent past. One institute used to formulate a framework programme every seventh year. It now defines research by projects and teams consisting of from five to seven researchers. Every research project is planned for a period of three to five years, at the end of which it is decided whether to continue the research, dissolve the team, or define a new project and/or team.

Barriers to effective management

Universities as well as government research institutes have generally improved their strategic planning and strengthened their managerial capacity. Certainly, there are differences across institutions and cultural difficulties for general acceptance of the rights of management. Danes, and apparently not least Danish researchers, oppose elitist attitudes and systems. Nevertheless, a trend towards such attitudes was noted in all interviews.

Two general problems challenge effective management at universities and government research institutes. One is the age profile of the research staff, which is dominated by researchers hired during the boom of the 1960s and 1970s. They are now between 45 and 55 years old. Few positions for younger researchers have opened up over the last 20 years so that, over the next ten to 20 years, most of these researchers will retire, leaving many positions for young researchers and few senior researchers to guide them.

Government schemes for the recruitment of researchers and incentives for increased production of PhDs have contributed to some extent to diminishing the age problem. At some institutions management has further contributed by deliberately offering incentives, sometimes not very favourable ones, for middle-aged researchers to leave the institutions. Still, the problem remains at most institutions, and interviewees welcome government initiatives for further reducing it, and normalising the age profile of institutional research staff.

Another problem is the low representation of women in research, and statistics show that, in the hierarchy of research positions, the share of women in total staff diminishes radically at the higher echelons. Some (male) managers of institutions identify this as a major problem for recruiting research managers in the future, when there will be a diminished population of senior researchers. Further, they point out that a number of managerial characteristics are closely linked to female characteristics [!!]. Government initiatives to balance the average research staff at institutions of research in this respect are also welcomed.

With respect to government research institutes, interviewees identified the structure of positions as a specific problem. A recent reform aims to harmonize the structure of positions at government research institutes and universities, except for professorships. Some interviewees argue that if government research institutes had professorships, they would attract more qualified researchers than at present, and mobility between these institutes and universities would improve. Others argue on the contrary that government research institutes could develop top positions more in line with their activities and more attractive than university professorships.

VI. THE BUSINESS ENTERPRISE SECTOR
AND RELATED POLICY

This chapter focuses on three major developments in the business enterprise sector and in related parts of the STI system. The first is the funding of research and development in the business enterprise sector; funding of the development of new products was a major political issue in the late 1980s, and two major funding institutions have been founded. The second is the restructuring of the approved technological service institutes (ATSIs). Finally it also discusses diffusion of knowledge across sectors of performance, first by summarising the general policy measures for improving diffusion discussed elsewhere, then by describing specific measures such as patenting, science parks, databases, and specific programmes for stimulating technology transfer.

1. Funding of business sector R&D

STI policy for the business enterprise sector is inseparable from government funding of STI activities.

Business enterprise expenditures on R&D are mainly funded by the companies themselves. In total, 83 per cent of the DKr 8 972 million spent on R&D by the business enterprises sector in 1991 was funded by companies and institutes themselves. Funding patterns differ strongly among sub-sectors (Table VI.1).

Companies in manufacturing industries fund no less than 92 per cent of their R&D by own sources. Government funds 4 per cent, of which half from the Ministry of Industry (in 1991, it allocated DKr 117 million to manufacturing companies). Other Danish firms fund 1 per cent of R&D by other firms, and 3 per cent of total funding is from abroad: in 1991, DKr 57 million came from EU programmes and DKr 114 million from other foreign sources.

Service companies have a somewhat different funding pattern. They only fund 81 per cent of their R&D themselves. As much as 6 per cent of their R&D is funded by other Danish firms and 4 per cent by EU programmes.

Technological service institutes have a very different funding pattern from that of service companies, with 14 per cent of their R&D funded from their own sources and 27 per cent funded by the Ministry of Industry in 1991. All together, 41 per cent of R&D

Table VI.1. **Funding of business sector R&D by source**

(percentages, 1991)

	Manufacturing firms	Service firms	Technological service institutes	Total
Own sources	92	81	14	83
External sources				
Ministry of Industry	2	2	27	4
Ministry of Research/National Research				
Councils	0	0	1	0
Other government schemes	2	1	13	2
Local Government Contract Research	0	2	0	1
Danish firms	1	6	24	4
Private organisations and funds	0	2	10	2
EU programmes	1	4	9	2
Other foreign sources	2	2	2	2
Total	100	100	100	100

Source: Ministry of Education, *Erhvervslivets forskning og udviklingsarbejde 1991*, Copenhagen.

performed by technological service institutes is paid for by government directly, while 45 per cent is funded either by Danish firms, organisations, and Funds or by sources abroad. EU programmes also play an important role for R&D performed by the technological service institutes; they accounted for 9 per cent of total funding in 1991.

Direct government funding of BERD plays a relatively small role in Denmark, as does funding from abroad. Even though funding of Danish BERD from abroad has risen since 1985 (an index of 397), funding from abroad is still much lower than for Norway and the United Kingdom (Table VI.2). However, funding from abroad has increased more for Denmark than for any other country analysed. Table IV.2 also shows that direct government funding has decreased in relative terms in all countries analysed, including Denmark. The decrease is especially dramatic in the United States, where direct government funding used to account for one-third of BERD.

Low, but increasing, R&D spending by Danish enterprises has raised the question of whether there are sufficient facilities for funding R&D, technology and innovation. In interviews with manufacturing firms, no clear trend was discernible. Some manufacturing firms emphasize that Danish industry is more dependent on innovation activities, especially implementation, than on R&D activities. On the other hand, enterprises have shown considerable interest in participating in strategic R&D programmes such as the Materials Technology Programme (MUP) and the Food Technology Programme (FØTEK).

In 1990, the Conservative-Liberal government reduced general corporate taxes from 50 to 40 per cent. Since then, the rates have been further reduced to 38-34 per cent. The idea was that a general tax reduction would avoid the need to stimulate specific industries

Table VI.2. Business enterprise expenditure on R&D by source of funds

(million national currencies, 1985-91, international comparison, index 1985 = 100)

	1985	1987	1989	1991
Denmark				
Business enterprise	100	125	147	191
Direct government	100	155	181	155
Private non-profit	100	368	500	511
Funds from abroad	100	139	202	397
Total	100	130	154	194
Norway				
Business enterprise	100	123	126	128
Direct government	100	133	134	134
Private non-profit	n.a.	n.a.	n.a.	n.a.
Funds from abroad	100	101	165	363
Total	100	125	128	135
Sweden				
Business enterprise	100	120	131	n.a.
Direct government	100	116	130	n.a.
Private non-profit	100	140	0	n.a.
Funds from abroad	100	156	191	n.a.
Total	100	120	132	n.a.
Netherlands				
Business enterprise	100	119	126	122[1]
Direct government	100	144	104	113[1]
Higher education	100	80	40	20[1]
Private non-profit	100	363	313	275[1]
Funds from abroad	100	82	143	90[1]
Total	100	121	124	120[1]
United Kingdom				
Business enterprise	100	128	157	160
Direct government	100	108	112	97
Funds from abroad	100	134	180	218
Total	100	124	149	152
Japan				
Business enterprise	100	109	139	165
Direct government	100	109	105	136
Private non-profit	100	138	54	77
Funds from abroad	100	100	133	167
Total	100	109	139	164
United States				
Business enterprise	100	108	124	134
Direct government	100	113	115	112
Total	100	109	121	127

1. 1990 figures.
Source: OECD, *Main Science and Technology Indicators 1993: 1,* Paris 1993.

or specific activities across industries. Accordingly, specific financial government support for STI activities in the business enterprise sector was reduced by DKr 1 billion.

Nonetheless, a specific tax reduction to stimulate participation in EU and EUREKA projects was introduced in 1987. In 1992, there was a further tax reduction to stimulate visits by high-ranking scientists from abroad. In addition, the Danish Fund for Industrial Growth was founded; it is largely a successor to the Industrial Research and Development Fund which was abolished in 1990 in order to finance the tax reductions. As a result, the intended changes in overall policies have, in fact, been rather small. Compared with other countries, however, Denmark has always had a rather low level of specific industry support, and this remains true. The general reduction in state funding of STI activities has primarily affected the technological service institutes, which were not compensated by the tax reduction as they do not pay taxes.

The general tendencies of intermediate policies, as seen from the different financing schemes, are that:

- in general, the state is reluctant to support specific industries;
- much emphasis is laid on incentives for co-operation between business enterprises and STI institutions;
- much emphasis is also placed on incentives to internationalise STI activities (see Chapter VIII).

Interviews indicate that the business enterprise sector has received these signals. According to interviews at the performing level, funding for business enterprise STI activities is not considered a major problem. The topic has received much political attention since the mid-1980s.

The funding of business sector STI is discussed below with respect to two new funding institutions: the Danish Development Finance Corporation and the Danish Fund for Industrial Growth.

The Danish Development Finance Corporation

The Danish Development Finance Corporation (DDFC) was founded as a limited company in 1988. Basically, it is a venture company with a share capital of DKr 500 million owned by a broad range of financial, institutional, and industrial investors. When it was formed, it was expected that other venture-capital companies and institutional investors would participate in many of its investments. This has not happened, largely because of the shift away from investment in new business activities that has occurred in Denmark and elsewhere since 1983, in large part because of the losses incurred by those providing venture capital.

DDFC has was had to play a larger role in financing individual portfolio companies than was originally intended, in terms of both the start-up and the follow-up investment which is inevitably needed. This tendency naturally intensified in 1992, because of the crisis in the financial sector, which also meant that, in some cases, DDFC has had to provide working capital in place of the banks.

DDFC has therefore intensified its efforts to acquire strategically-relevant sources of investment and business partners for its portfolio companies in order to widen the ownership base for a number of the companies in its investment portfolio. These efforts have also to be seen as an element of DDCF's exit strategy. DDFC's business concept is to help develop new ventures to a commercially-interesting level. Once this has been achieved, its task is essentially over, and it is thereafter for other investors to develop the company.

The Danish Fund for Industrial Growth

In 1992, the Ministry of Industry established the Danish Fund for Industrial Growth with an initial capital of DKr 2 billion. The Fund is a self-governing institution with a board of directors which includes five representatives from industry. Its main target group is private enterprises with less than 250 employees and less than DKr 150 million in annual turnover. Larger enterprises can, however, receive appropriations for technological development projects. The Fund also offers counselling in connection with appropriations to individual projects.

The idea behind the Fund was to offer small and medium-sized enterprises better possibilities for technological development and international marketing. When the Industrial Research and Development Fund, the Product Development Scheme, and the Market Development Scheme were cancelled in 1990, a funding vacuum resulted, and the Fund was established in order to stimulate process, product, and market development projects and thereby create economic growth among small and medium-sized enterprises. In order to do this, the Fund supports promising projects that are financially risky.

As of 24 June 1993, the Fund had co-funded more than 100 development projects and 107 private enterprises for a total of DKr 170 million. Most funding has been given as loans to technological development projects with a long-term perspective, although the appropriations increasingly go to market development projects. Furthermore, the loans mainly go to high/advanced technology development. As a result of the increasing number of applications, the Fund has received the right to use, in addition to its annual return, part of its basic capital for appropriations. The Fund may co-fund a maximum of DKr 350 million annually.

Most of the enterprises that have received appropriations are small, but the number of medium-sized firms applying for financial support is rising. In the year 1993, 22 per cent of the appropriations were given to enterprises (with 10-19 employees), 27 per cent went to enterprises with 20-49 employees, and 39 per cent to enterprises with over 50 employees.

On the basis of interviews, it appears that for equity funding of business development, including STI activities, there are fewer good projects and ideas than sources of funding. Risk loan funding offered by the Danish Fund for Industrial Growth, instead, seems very attractive to companies and now funds around 200 new companies a year. The interviewees thus indirectly question the need for new funding facilities such as the development institutions proposed by the Government in autumn 1993.

More directly, interviewees raise the question of how the funding institutions interact with the other institutions and overall strategies of the STI system. The Fund for Industrial Growth sees no obligation to follow the general strategic views of the Industry and Trade Development Council; its funding strategy is very project- and market-oriented. Formal interaction between the Fund's board and the Industry and Trade Development Council is limited, but informal exchanges on general trends and strategies are more extensive.

2. The approved technological service institutes and relevant policy

The 1987 OECD review recommended, in particular, a simplification of the administration of the ATSIs. As a result of restructuring, their number has dropped from 36 in the mid-1980s to 14 at the end of 1994. Furthermore, the number of administrators has been reduced, and the management of the scheme has been strengthened. Interviewees see the operation as generally successful, even though a number of problems remain.

Six of the ATSIs, which represent almost 60 per cent of the turnover of the scheme, have economic problems. Low liquidity and cash flow problems force management to focus on measures that ensure short-term income. If the ATSIs are to fulfil their objectives, management must concentrate on the strategic level with a medium-term horizon. In many institutes, the board of directors has been concentrating more on technical development than on business management.

It is seen as important to strengthen overall STI strategy, as well as independence and managerial capacity within institutions, and to stress dissemination in strategic programmes. It also appears worthwhile to consider affiliating venture-capital facilities with all the science parks, to conduct a national campaign on the advantages derived from using database facilities, and to re-introduce a specific Technology Transfer Programme.

The Industry and Trade Development Council and the Danish Agency for Development of Industry and Trade manage the ATSIs, which are funded in part by the state. The ATSI scheme is an important part of intermediate STI policy; its purpose is to provide technological services within a wide range of technical areas, with special attention to small and medium-sized enterprises (SMEs).

Participating institutes are independent non-profit entities managed by a board of directors appointed by the Danish Academy of Technical Sciences, whereas in other institutes, the board of directors is typically appointed by a council. Participating institutes must obtain approval from the Minister of Industry, and recommendations for approval are given by the Industry and Trade Development Council. Approval is normally given for five years, with a professional evaluation of the institutes' activities every three years.

Each year the Industry and Trade Development Council decides how basic funding from the state budget is to be distributed among the approved institutes. In principle, it announces to individual institutes the level of funding for a three-year period. Despite current reductions in basic funding from the state budget, total turnover in participating institutes has been increasing over the last ten years.

Figure VI.1. **The interaction between the ATSIs and their clients and suppliers**

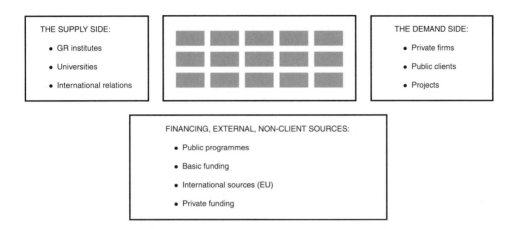

THE SUPPLY SIDE:
- GR institutes
- Universities
- International relations

THE DEMAND SIDE:
- Private firms
- Public clients
- Projects

FINANCING, EXTERNAL, NON-CLIENT SOURCES:
- Public programmes
- Basic funding
- International sources (EU)
- Private funding

Although clients furnish most of the financing, extramural financing – 13 per cent basic funding and 27 per cent project funding in 1992 – has a significant impact. The interaction between ATSIs and their clients and suppliers is illustrated in Figure VI.1, which shows the major elements (the supply side, the demand side, and the financing). Other aspects are the strategies of individual institutes and the R&D performed from basic funding in order to upgrade the institute's knowledge base.

The type of demand is obviously a decisive factor in the development of the ATSIs. It is important, for instance, for institutes to be able to choose their assignments to some extent to ensure that they fit into the institution's strategy. The supply side is also important for the development of the ATSIs. Knowledge is bought on the market but is also acquired through national and international co-operation with researchers. Finally, project financing has an important impact. In the national programmes, there has recently been a tendency to create larger and broader programmes in order to engage in national and international co-operation. The balance between short-term, medium-term and long-term financing has an impact as well. Basic financing is in principle medium-term (three-year periods), and much financing is short-term. Participation in STI programmes results in output for customers and input for internal knowledge production.

In 1982, there were 36 approved institutes but in 1992 the number had dropped to 18 and was to be reduced to 14 in 1994 because of a structural reorganisation which will be described below. The ATSIs include three groups of institutes: the Danish Technological Institute (DTI), the Danish Academy of Technical Sciences (ATV) institute, and others. The DTI represents more than a third of the total activity (37 per cent); it has six divisions, each of which has its own sectoral board.

The management of the ATSIs

Within the Ministry of Industry, the Danish Agency for Development of Industry and Trade administers and monitors the ATSI scheme. The Agency's main activities are: developing the scheme, recommending approval of institutes and allocations of basic funding to institutes, ensuring regular professional evaluations, and exercising financial supervision (control).

Basic financing is the main means by which the Industry and Trade Development Council and the Danish Agency for Development of Industry and Trade influence the development of individual institutes (financing to build competence), ensure co-ordination among institutes, and create joint strategies.

The Council and the Agency are assisted by an advisory committee, the ATSI Committee, appointed in October 1993, which acts as a steering committee for the regular professional evaluations of the ATSIs and for the financial control function. Among other things the Advisory Committee will examine the evaluations of the services provided by the ATSIs, their strategic plans, the analyses of their economic situation, the need for structural improvements in the system, and the boundaries between institutes in the system.

The Agency has also established an evaluation unit, which will systematise the professional evaluations, using both internal and external human resources. A second unit, designed to ensure financial control of ATSI activities, has also been established as a service to the institutes.

Policy relating to the ATSI scheme

In co-operation with the Agency for Development of Industry and Trade, the Industry and Trade Development Council – which replaced the Technology Council in 1990 but did not change its policies or strategies – develops policy and joint strategies for the ATSI scheme.

During the ten years from 1982 to 1992, the state budget accorded the ATSI scheme diminishing priority. As noted above, in 1992 state funding was 13 per cent of total turnover. Throughout the years 1988-94, the Industry and Trade Development Council's main objective has been to ensure satisfactory utility value, through improved management and strategic planning, from state funding.

One measure designed to improve utility value has been market orientation; ATSI services are not to be subsidised through state funding but sold to clients, including the small and medium-sized enterprises, at market prices. To achieve this objective, basic funding has been directed towards the reinforcement of knowledge and skills in the ATSIs.

The main measure for achieving improved utility value, however, has been the structural reorganisation undertaken by the Danish Agency for Development of Industry and Trade and the advisory bodies from 1989 to 1994. Its goals were to concentrate resources on a smaller number of professional units, reduce overlapping technological competencies in participating institutes, ensure a more stable financial status, increase users' influence on the institutes' activities, and increase international awareness of the institutes.

The Industry and Trade Development Council has encouraged the ATSIs to establish joint representation (with larger user involvement). Not all institutes have seen the need for such a body, and it has not yet been established.

Restructuring the ATSIs

The restructuring of the ATSI scheme (1989-93) reduced the number of participating legal entities from 36 to 14 (during 1994). The number of professional and economic/ funding units was reduced from around 60 to 20. Changes are indicated in Figure VI.2 (the Geotechnical Institute, which was not involved in the merger activities, is not included).

The merger process is at different stages in different institutes. The necessary internal changes have been characterised by the wish for integration. Organisational integration has occurred to a great extent. However, in terms of location, integration has been more difficult in some cases, owing to the prohibitive cost of moving laboratories and technical equipment. The results of interviews suggest that, from the viewpoint of the institutes, the mergers have been successful, and a number of institutes have found new

Figure VI.2. **The restructuring of the STI system**

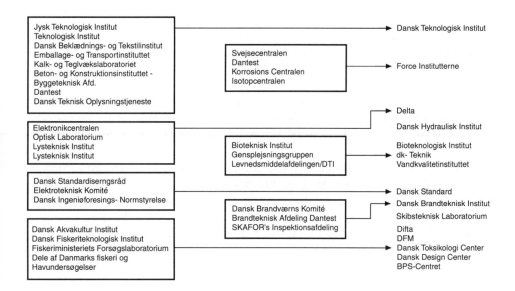

synergies. The policy level is not fully satisfied with the results. They see the restructuring as an ongoing process and look forward to the results of the work of the ATSI Committee.

The two largest institutes represent 55 per cent of total turnover, and co-operation among participating institutes is affected by this lack of balance. To improve both the balance among institutes and their management, the possibility of splitting up the largest institute while maintaining the advantages of physical proximity has been considered.

Economic problems and stable financing

Some of the aims of the restructuring have not been achieved. A main problem is that six of the approved institutes, which represent almost 60 per cent of total turnover, have rather severe economic problems, particularly in terms of liquidity. As a result, the management of the affected institutes has turned to means of ensuring short-term income. Yet, in order to fulfil the objectives of the scheme, management must concentrate on the strategic level and a medium-term horizon. Economic problems therefore interfere with efforts to realise strategic objectives.

A number of explanations have been given for the economic situation of the ATSIs: the reduction of basic funding and the increase in programme funding, market pricing of services to all clients, competition with governmental research institutes whose basic funding is much better, the general recession, the unexpectedly high cost of merging institutes, and unsatisfactory management.

The ATSIs themselves stress that financing projects through the strategic programmes is causing difficulties, because of what is often a stop-and-go policy for the programmes, which makes it very difficult to use capacity satisfactorily. On the other hand, ATSI interviews confirm the impression given by interviews with private companies that the strategic programmes have resulted in broader co-operation between the two. It could also be assumed that the increase in programme financing, especially through EU programmes, has promoted both the internationalisation and the growth of ATSI R&D activities since the mid-1980s.

Another explanation of the economic difficulties of the ATSIs may be the reduction of basic funding. The ATSIs are generally reluctant to point this out as the essential problem. There does not appear to be any well-motivated official justification for the reduction of state funding.

SMEs criticise market pricing of services and claim that it has created barriers to their use of ATSI services and led them to reduce their use of these services.

Those at the policy level stress that the general management of the ATSIs has to be improved and that the institutes should have responded earlier to their economic problems. They emphasize that the current economic problems show that management must be further improved. From a different perspective, they too see reduced basic funding as a problem: "We pay enough for what we get, but we should get more and pay more."

The idea of moving the financing of the ATSI scheme out of the state budget and creating a fund with a basic capital (a parallel to the Danish Fund for Industrial Growth), which would, from its returns, finance the ATSIs was discussed during the interviews. In general, those at the policy level find that the level of basic financing for the government research institutes and the ATSIs is out of proportion.

The management of the institutes

In the interviews, many pointed out that unsatisfactory management is part of the severe economic problem. In many institutes, the board of directors has concentrated more on technical development than on business management. A number of institutes must redirect their management to make it more strategic and business-oriented.

Increased attention has been given to strategic planning in the past years, and the institutes have given higher priority to strategic planning. Opinions differ on the results. Both the policy level and the performing level express satisfaction but note that results resemble long-term budgeting rather than strategic planning. However, awareness has been increased.

ATSIs interviewed welcome the newly-formed ATSI Committee. In terms of evaluation and economic control, the Committee is accepted as a new partner for institutes in the effort to determine whether the structure of institutes matches the needs of the market.

Those interviewed at the policy level feel that the restructuring has not met all their objectives concerning management. For instance, the idea of creating a superstructure for the ATSIs has not been discarded. The ATSIs today are still split into three groups, DTI, the ATV institutes, and others. Policy level representatives see the ATSI Committee as an important tool in the restructuring process but not as the final solution to an inadequate structure.

Challenges for the future

The ATSI scheme is considered very important to Danish industrial innovation policy. Research, statistical analysis, and interviews make it possible to identify several key strategic issues. They are chosen because they were brought out by a considerable number of the persons interviewed and because they are of strategic importance for the general development of the scheme.

Strengthening ATSI management

The requirements for the board of directors of ATSIs do not differ significantly from those for the board in commercial companies. It must manage the overall organisation, strategies, business plans, investments, etc. Shortcomings are generally on the business side, as the boards have typically paid greater attention to the technological side of their activities. Over the last five to ten years, improvements have been made, but in general the boards have not yet put effort into executive management, especially in the business areas, a view generally expressed at the policy level. Most of the executive managers interviewed at the performing level confirmed this view.

Unsatisfactory financial basis

Given the amount of basic funding for the ATSI scheme, the institutes are dependent on income from programmes and clients. The combination of reduced basic funding and increased programme funding (with much self-financing) has caused problems, notably due to stop-and-go policies. As a number of the institutes have an unsatisfactory level of equity capital, they find themselves in a situation where it is difficult to maintain the necessary long-term horizon for building up competencies.

If their financial problems are not solved, it will be difficult for these institutes to differentiate themselves from private consulting firms and maintain their profile and their role in industrial innovation policy. Ensuring satisfactory equity capital in these institutes is therefore another strategic key issue.

Strategic planning

The main aims of restructuring were to reduce the overlap between the institutes and to match the structure of institutes with the evolution towards larger firms in the business enterprise sector. It seemed irrational for the state to support the development of knowledge and skills in the same areas in different institutions. Whereas reduction of overlap has been a main issue in intermediate policies for the institutes, no attempt has been made to develop an overall strategic plan for the scheme.

During the last two years the Industry and Trade Development Council has completed analyses of the financial status of eight resource areas in the Danish business enterprise sector. The analyses, which cover around 90 per cent of all Danish industry and trade, identify the conditions that will determine future development and innovation by enterprises in these areas.

These analyses offer an interesting basis for specific strategic planning for the ATSI scheme. Questions which might enter into play for the programming of a strategic process include: How does the priority of resources fit into objectives and/or the recognised needs? Are the right areas being covered, or have gaps developed? Does the scheme primarily serve R&D institutes or industrial innovation? What are its main objectives? The ATSI Committee has begun to consider these issues.

3. Dissemination of technology

Improving the efficiency and competitiveness of the STI system is to a large extent a question of how quickly research results and knowledge are transmitted and disseminated through the STI system and from there to users in society. Dissemination also enhances the ability of the overall STI system to respond to scientific and technological challenges.

Following a review of the general measures for disseminating knowledge both within the STI system and from there to its users, specific measures such as patenting, databases, and science parks are described.

General measures

One of the main features of the STI system and its development since 1987 has been the widespread use of strategic programmes, which have had a positive effect on the STI system as regards to its ability to convey and disseminate information and knowledge throughout the system (see Chapter IV). According to interviewees, the cross-council/ministerial R&D programmes have strengthened interaction between different parts of the STI system, and thus contributed to greater exchange of research results and knowledge.

Early programmes, such as the Action Plan for Research and Development (FTU), were criticised for insufficient co-operation between the research community and private enterprises, partly owing to scarce administrative resources. A "mid-period" programme, such as the Food Technology Programme I (FØTEK I), suffered to some extent from the division of the administration among different ministries. Yet most of the programme's difficulties were overcome by a co-ordination committee, and the lessons learned led to the establishment of a joint administrative body for the implementation of the Environmental Research Programme. The administration of the Materials Technology Development Programme (MUP), which includes both researchers and users of research, has proven to be another successful way of conducting strategic programmes.

Still, a number of interviewees point to obstacles to dissemination, due primarily to "cultural" and "structural" differences between performers of STI activities in different sectors. These differences reflect different attitudes towards STI activities. At universities, STI activities are often seen as their own end, the objective being to gain and make available new knowledge. In government research institutes, attitudes are often very similar, as neither the institutes nor the researchers and scientists have a specific interest in the commercial exploitation of their results. Companies and, to some extent, technological service institutes, are more interested in exploiting STI results than in performing the STI activities as such.

Evaluations of specific national scientific fields have improved coherence in the STI system, and organisational restructuring has facilitated dissemination. At present, national strategies are being developed for both agricultural and health research. There is no doubt that dissemination will be facilitated in the long run by the establishment of such national strategies.

National strategies need to be co-ordinated into an overall strategy if optimal conditions for dissemination are to be established. This raises the question of how to organise ministerial responsibility for the STI system as well as how to organise the top-level policy advisory structure discussed in Chapter III.

Specific measures

While the general measures for enhancing dissemination are most important, since they affect the basic conditions for interaction within the STI system, specific measures play an important role as well. This section reviews some of the principal ones: patenting, science parks, databases, and specific programme activities.

Patenting

Patenting and licensing furnish a common ground for universities and government research institutes when they co-operate with technological service institutes and companies on joint STI projects. They are therefore an important way of spreading research results.

However, university researchers have a low patenting frequency, and very few government research institutes have taken out patents or submitted patent applications in Denmark in recent years. Given their considerable share of research, and of applications-oriented research performed by government research institutes, their patenting rate is clearly low.

There are many reasons for this, among them inadequate awareness of patent rights in general and existing service possibilities in particular, complex tax rules, resource-intensive procedures, unclear legal situation as regards patent rights, and a lack of tradition and knowledge about patenting and licensing.

In other words, researchers do not feel that they have enough incentive to approach potential buyers or partners on their own, nor do the research institutions have sufficient incentive to involve themselves in the process.

Interviewees did not suggest any specific ways of improving patenting and licensing by universities and government research institutions as a mechanism for disseminating STI results within the STI system. National campaigns to increase attention of researchers, scientists, as well as institutions, to these issues have met with little success. Strengthening the independence and managerial capacity of institutions and including patents and licences in evaluation criteria might improve the incentives for both individuals and institutions.

Science parks

Another way to improve dissemination is to encourage universities and companies to co-operate in science parks. No interviewees claimed that lack of co-operation is due to legal or institutional barriers between companies and universities, whereas only a few years ago the governing rules of universities would have been identified as the dominant obstacle.

In Denmark, five science parks were established in the period 1986-92 and these have close ties with the country's universities. Thus, they are regionally-based bodies whose function is to promote the growth and development of the region's knowledge-based companies and organisations, and to support and promote entrepreneurial activities among researchers. The knowledge that exists in the region's science centres and universities is used in co-operative efforts, on market terms, between the companies and the various institutions of the regional research community.

A major function of science parks is to act as an incubator for the development of small new knowledge-based companies. Apart from providing office space and operational facilities for participating parties, the science parks promote and procure different forms of co-operation, ranging from the exchange of information on an informal basis to the signing of contracts for consulting assistance.

The science parks have widely varying organisational and economic structures, and to a certain extent different strengths, depending on the nearby universities and the trade and industry structure of the region.

The present Government intends to propose a bill, which, among other things, will extend the legal empowerment of county and district authorities to support science parks.

Interviewees argue that science parks could more effectively fulfil their mission if they had the necessary venture capital. At present, only one Danish science park has venture capital at its disposal, although experience abroad clearly indicates that the presence of venture capital makes science parks better able to exploit results and knowledge. Consequently, it is worthwhile considering how such facilities might be affiliated to all the science parks.

Databases

A third way to improve dissemination is to establish databases for making the knowledge of the STI system available. In co-operation with the National Library Service, the National Committee for Scientific and Technical Information and Documentation (DANDOK), assists the Government and public authorities with the overall organisation of policy in the area of information, with special reference to scientific and technical and market information. DANDOK operates the DANDOK database, which contains information on research projects and publications at a number of Danish research institutions and programmes.

DANDOK has recently presented a proposal for a more flexible and more efficient information policy. The fundamental element in the prospective policy is to give high priority to the expansion and quality assurance of the database of Danish research, which will be centralised in the rather long term. The DANDOK database already contains about 60 000 records, with information on ongoing and published research at Danish research institutions. The aim is to make the overview complete as quickly as possible.

Infoscan (formerly the Danish DIANE Centre) is a national centre under the Ministry of Research. Its function is to inform and advise Danish research, administration, trade and industry on electronic information services, including access to, and use of, on-line databases. The European Commission has designated Infoscan as a "National Awareness Partner" for the IMPACT II programme and, at the same time, the centre has become an agent for the EU's Eurobases. Infoscan has information and advice on all the databases of the European Commission.

Interviews indicate that the present database facilities are appropriate and sufficient. A national campaign to improve knowledge of the database facilities might be considered, but interviews point mainly to a cultural barrier for increased use of the facilities by companies. Interviewees noted that it is often thought that knowledge that is accessible to everybody in databases is less valuable from a commercial point of view.

Technology transfer from abroad

Dissemination can also be improved by specific programmes. A Technology Transfer Programme, administered by the Academy for Technical Sciences, was implemented in 1987 by the Agency for Development of Trade and Industry and abolished in 1989. The programme aimed to give financial support to Danish enterprises for the procurement of advanced technical knowledge. The financing of the programme depended on co-funding of key employees stationed abroad for a period of from three months to three years. During the three-year programme, 61 Danish enterprises received total funds of DKr 25 million for stationing 812 employees in 15 different countries.

A 1992 evaluation report of the Technology Transfer Programme concluded that the programme was a success for the enterprises that participated. In many cases the know-how acquired by enterprises was transferred into new or improved products and services and, not surprisingly, the enterprises expressed their disappointment when the programme was terminated in 1989. In their 1992 report, the Academy recommended a continuation of the programme. Accordingly, the appropriateness of re-establishing a Technology Transfer Programme should be considered.

VII. TECHNOLOGY ASSESSMENT AND ETHICS

The belief that science, research and technology are strictly positive factors in economic and social development was increasingly questioned during the late 1970s and early 1980s, and criticism was quite strong in wealthy countries such as Denmark. Great attention was paid to the way technology affects job content, the environment, lifestyles, and various aspects of everyday life, and science and research were criticised for taking insufficient account of the ethical aspects of their activities.

New technologies of the last decades, such as informatics and biotechnology, have given rise to demands for assessment, ethical analysis, and public debate. Especially since 1993, government policy has aimed at strengthening the integration of technology assessment (TA) and ethics into the STI system and into society as a whole. Growing internationalisation may play a role, given that a Danish competitive advantage is the ability to transform social values into products. Products of high ethical, environmental, and social quality may well be the result of a successful integration of assessment into the STI system.

Since the mid-1980s, some institutionalisation of TA and ethics has taken place in Denmark, although diffusion and integration of TA and ethics throughout the STI system and STI activities remains limited. The Danish Board of Technology, established in 1985, has initiated and followed technology assessment and developed a model of parliamentary TA that integrates assessment and public debate. Ethical assessment with respect to science, technology, and innovation has been institutionalised in the Danish Council of Ethics, in the system of scientific ethics committees, and in the Council of Animal Ethics and the Council of Animal Tests.

As regards the actual diffusion and integration of both TA and ethics, it is important to distinguish between two groups of STI actors. The first and largest consists of the STI institutions which are outside the assessment institutions; while they view assessments positively, very few have made assessment part of their routines or strategies. The second group consists of actors from and close to assessment institutions for TA and ethics; their experience and knowledge is naturally greater, as is their insight into problems and solutions for the integration of TA and ethics into the STI system.

This chapter presents technology assessment and ethics as objectives on the overall STI policy agenda. Especially since 1993, strengthening and integration of technology assessment and ethics in actual science, technology, and innovation is an issue that has come to the fore. The discussion first notes the major institutional developments in the fields of technology assessment and ethics. It then focuses on barriers to diffusion and integration into STI activities, which are related to know-how, independence, strategy, unstable funding, and the lack of regulations. Finally, on the basis of interviews, different ways of securing further diffusion and integration of technology assessment and ethics into STI activities are discussed. Among them are technology forecasting and priority setting, assessment services, university assessment centres, integration of technology assessment and ethics in university curricula, and legal requirements for using assessments.

1. Technology assessment

The institutionalisation of technology assessment in Denmark takes four main forms:
- *Expert assessments.* TA is traditionally performed by experts, who review facts, assess impact of current or alternative developments, propose action or strategies or assess their consequences. The research methods used are often traditional but may be multi-disciplinary.
- *Party-oriented assessments*, either advocacy or action research. Advocacy research assumes that TA is not neutral and should be carried out by the interested parties. The assessor plays the role of spokesman and describes problems and develops actions for the group, using interviews, questionnaires, bibliographical research, and reference groups. Action research assumes that it is easier to make changes with people than for them. The researcher acts as member of the group and supports its analysis and policy. Methods used include workshops, future labs.
- *Participatory TA.* Grass-roots organisations, labour market organisations, experts, and lay people engage in dialogue within the framework of the project in order to reshape technologies, make statements, develop strategies, or act. Participatory TA works across disciplines and interest groups, using negotiation and dialogue – social experiments with new technologies, consensus conferences, etc.
- *Informed opinion or mediated TA.* Assessments are made by the participants themselves on a basis of communication products and debate and are an aspect of the regular democratic process. The assessor creates communication products and facilitates the debate. Methods used are media strategies, communication products, and debates. Because of Denmark's long tradition of using this process for all social issues (''people's enlightenment''), it has been naturally integrated into Danish TA.

The role, institutionalisation, and methodology of TA have been discussed in Denmark since the early 1980s. The resulting development can be grossly characterised as a movement from the first two to the latter two forms. Dialogue and debate have increasingly furnished the basis for shaping statements, defining needs and demands, and formulating a common basis for new plans and actions. They have become the main tools for creating common and comprehensive understanding of technology, its consequences, and the available choices. At the same time, efforts to avoid conflict in this area have increased. According to interviewees, this evolution has helped give Danish TA a more constructive reputation, and more credibility.

TA has become a part of major R&D programmes such as the Technology Development Programme (TUP), the Food Technology Programme (FØTEK), and the Biotechnological R&D Programme I (BIOTEK). Participatory TA and management-oriented TA have been supported by the Ministry of Industry and the health care sector, among others. In the TUP, the industry concerned often co-financed the projects, but the government was still the main source of funding. During the last five years, there has been much less TA in R&D programmes, where it is present at all.

In connection with the research councils, social/technological research has had its own institution. The programme funded projects, most of which had an applied TA profile, for a total of DKr 22 million. Since the end of this initiative, funding from the research councils is much more limited, and the projects funded are more oriented towards theory and methodology. Also, some trade unions have established internal technology consulting functions, but very few TA projects have been initiated by the trade unions.

Danish participatory TA is unique. During the past last couple of years institutions in Italy, Switzerland, Belgium, Britain, Norway, Sweden, the Netherlands, the United States and the European Union have shown great interest in learning from Danish experience and adopting some of these methods.

In general, interviewees did not question the validity of this methodological approach. However, few of them knew very much about TA methodology. Some interviewees felt that TA and ethics are difficult to assess when dealing with basic science, and others felt that while the use of gene technology, for example, can be assessed, it is more difficult to assess new materials and information technology.

In 1985, the Danish Parliament (*Folketinget*) established the Danish Board of Technology (*TeknologiNævnet*). The Board's role is to initiate and monitor technology assessment and promote public debate on the consequences of technology for society and the individual citizen. It is attached directly to the Parliament through a nine-member committee composed of members of Parliament, and it is under the authority of the Ministry of Research. The Board itself consists of 15 members from different parts of society who are personally appointed by the Minister of Research on the basis of suggestions from the nine-member committee, counties and municipalities, trade unions, employers' organisations, the Consumers Council, the Technology Council, the adult education network, and the research councils.

In December 1989, the Parliament voted a new five-year period, which will end in July 1995. The Board now has a budget of DKr 9 million per year. The Danish Board of Technology Act stipulates that the legislation should be reviewed by Parliament no later than the parliamentary year 1994-95.

There are two opposing ideas about the future role of the Board. One is that there should be a stronger connection to Parliament and more work devoted to analysis (along the lines of the US Office of Technology Assessment). The other is that it should focus on local experiments and the funding of local debate (the informed opinion model).

Persons interviewed do not oppose the existence and function of The Danish Board of Technology, nor do they propose a change in the methodological approach. On the contrary, some emphasized the credibility of the existing model – an independent body with analytic as well as participatory approaches and responsibility for public debate.

2. Ethics

Since research has become an increasingly social matter, questions about the relationship of research to the norms and values of society arise. In Denmark, the issue of ethics came to the forefront in the mid-1980s in connection with public debate on changes in hereditary features of plants, animals, and humans through genetic engineering. Public reaction was the background first to a very restrictive Act on genetic engineering and second to a request from the scientific community itself for ethical guidelines in different areas.

The interviews have shown that both scientists and administrators see the need for ethical assessments and an open debate on some developments in biotechnology. All levels of the STI system seem to be aware of the need for more public acceptance of some research areas. On the other hand, as noted above, some interviewees see areas such as new materials and information technology difficult or unnecessary to assess ethically.

The first institutional response to ethical concerns was the formation of the Danish Council of Ethics, established by statute of Parliament in 1987. The Council consists of 17 members, eight of whom are appointed by the Minister of Health and nine by a dedicated parliamentary nine-member committee; most are experts in philosophy, ethics, biology, or medicine. The Council's domain is ethical issues in biomedicine. One of its tasks is to submit proposals for legislation for the protection of fertilised human ova, embryos, and foetuses; it also advises the Government on the issue of genetic manipulation of human gametes used for fertilisation. Another of its functions is to inform the public and promote debate on ethics and biomedicine. The Council has issued debate materials and information in various forms and has held meetings on issues such as the definition of death, the protection of fertilised human ova, embryos and foetuses, the registration of sensitive personal data, and genetic engineering. Furthermore, it funds local debate arrangements.

In 1992, the Parliament passed an Act on a system of scientific ethics committees for biomedical research projects. This inaugurated a formal system for approving research projects involving experiments with humans, foetuses, or human cells. (The system had in fact functioned on a voluntary basis among medical researchers since the end of the 1970s.) The system consists of seven regional committees as well as the Central Scientific Ethics Committee of Denmark, all of which are composed of both laymen and researchers. All Danish biomedical research projects involving experimentation with human beings and with human cells, foetuses, and tissues must be reported to, and approved by, the Regional Scientific Ethics Committee. The Central Scientific Ethics Committee serves as board of appeal. The committees ensure that projects involve no unreasonable risks, that the subjects involved have given their informed consent, and that the projects maintain high scientific standards. In addition, both the regional and the central committees promote public debate on general issues in biomedical research.

The Danish Council for Animal Experiments, which is responsible for the Danish Animal Experiment Inspection Authority, has been established to monitor experiments involving animals. Animal experimentation is regulated by the Act on Animal Experiments. Experiments with animals which can be assumed to cause the animal pain, suffering, or permanent damage may only be conducted with the permission of the Animal Experiment Inspection Authority.

The Danish Ethical Council for Animals, under the auspices of the Ministry of Justice, was established in January 1992 in accordance with the Act on the Protection of Animals. It is the Council's duty to monitor developments in animal protection on the basis of ethical evaluation.

In 1992, the Danish Medical Research Council established the Committee on Scientific Misconduct, which deals with cases of alleged misconduct in health research. It takes up such cases either on request or at its own initiative.

In 1993, the Danish Social Science Research Council established the Committee on Ethics in the Social Sciences. Its task up to the beginning of 1994 was to identify ethical issues in the various social sciences.

Both in Denmark and abroad, there are codes of professional ethics in many fields. In Denmark, for example, doctors and lawyers have ethical rules. In October 1993, the Danish Association of Lawyers and Economists published a report on principles of professional ethics in public administration, including draft guidelines for a set of ethical rules for civil servants.

The research councils' strategy plans of 1992 indicated a need for research on fundamental bioethical problems. Five of the six research councils allocated a total of DKr 15 million to research on bioethics. The money was awarded to two interdisciplinary research groups, which will conduct research in 1993-97 on the problems associated with the development and application of biotechnology both within and outside the human area.

The interviews indicate that, besides the procedures for approving experiments, there is little ongoing dialogue between the STI system and the ethics institutions. One interviewee argued that ethical analysis should never be a routine procedure but should be undertaken when a need or a problem is recognised. This point of view differs from the more strategic point of view that assessment activities should be carried out before problems arise or in order to reveal needs. The interviewee in question might take a more strategic approach if more participatory methods were introduced into the work of the institutions.

3. Further diffusion and integration of technology assessment and ethics into STI activities

According to interviews, further diffusion and integration of assessment, both technology assessment and ethical assessment, and advising, face five different barriers: know-how, independence, strategy, unstable funding, lack of regulations.

The know-how barrier. The STI system generally is ignorant of the potential of assessment and its methods, and this may be a problem for integrating assessment into the system. Interviews of the large group of persons from outside the assessment institutions show that there is very little understanding of assessment methodology and practice. TA and ethics are generally regarded as difficult to apply to basic science. Nevertheless, some credit is given to the assessment system, and gene technology is given as an example of a research area that public debate has made it easier to deal with.

The independence barrier. If STI researchers do the assessments themselves, the issue of credibility arises, and integration of assessment may not occur if research institutions or scientists are responsible. Generally, interviews showed that it should not be the responsibility of researchers to ensure that assessments are carried out. A managing director of a large research institution stated that it is not for the research institution to assess whether a technology should be used. Once a technology is developed, decision on its use is the responsibility of politicians and public debate. The need for cross-disciplinary assessments and the fact that the researcher cannot be objective mean that assessment should be performed by others.

The strategy barrier. If technological and ethical assessments are not undertaken in connection with the formulation and administration of R&D programmes, there is a risk that R&D strategies will be defined on scientific criteria alone, leaving aside parameters which concern socio-economics, ethics, environment, working conditions, quality of life, etc. The strategy problem is summed up by the question, "What is a suitable science and technology policy?" According to interview results, however, TA and ethics are generally not part of the planning and administration of R&D programmes. One ministry agency which always evaluates socio-economic and environmental effects of programmes and projects is an exception to the rule. One interviewee stated that assessments are often based on subjective ethical values, a fact which can be problematic when formulating a suitable technology policy. Other interviewees stressed the need for objectives, criteria of success, and vision for overall science policy.

Unstable funding barrier. Rapidly changing funding for assessment research impedes the incorporation of assessment expertise into STI institutions, as both institutions and researchers are uncertain about future funding of assessment activities. If integrating ethics and TA into research institutions is an objective, the lack of long-lasting local initiatives presents a problem. Funding for TA research through R&D programmes and the research councils has diminished over the last five years. In contrast, according to the interviews, funding for ethical assessments seems to have become more available. One interviewee expressed a wish for more continuity in order to ensure a steady development of theory and methods, and attract experts and students.

Lack of regulations barrier. No decision-makers are obliged to use assessments, so that assessments tend to remain on the sidelines in decision-making rather than be an integrated part of it. The expectations, motivation, and credibility of assessment suffer as a result. Denmark has some good examples of assessment by decision-makers on different levels. As in other countries, however, the general impression is that assessments are little used. This creates some problems. First, the STI system can continue to develop technologies, and expect society to take care of any subsequent problems. Second, the public may see assessments in the long run only as legitimation and without real significance. Third, assessors' motivation is diminished if they do not expect their findings to be used.

In Sweden, the Netherlands, England, Spain, France, Canada, and Australia, TA is a regulative precondition for decision-making on the implementation of new technologies in the health care sector. In Denmark, it is voluntary. One interviewee saw this as the main problem for further development of the assessment system.

4. Policy options

Interviews, particularly with persons with insight into TA and ethics, propose the following options.

Option 1: A technology-forecasting and priority-setting function

In order to strengthen the strategic basis for the formulation and administration of government R&D programmes, a priority-setting procedure which integrates technological and ethical assessments could be developed.

The model for such a procedure might be practices in other countries, such as the "Future Technologies" analysis in Japan and the bibliometric methods discussed in Chapter V. Priority setting could be developed as a hybrid of the Japanese "Strategic Conferences" and the Danish dialogue-oriented methods, which can include parameters such as ethics, economics, social consequences, and the environment.

If implemented, such a function would weaken central parts of the strategy barrier. The independence barrier would also be weakened to some extent because part of the necessary assessments would occur outside the research institutions before the R&D programmes were launched.

Option 2: An assessment service function

An assessment service function would give researchers the possibility of initiating assessments and debate on the results and consequences of scientific projects. Because of the freedom of scientific research to choose its scientific objectives, the research institution, the researcher, or the general public may find ethical assessment and advice and technology assessment necessary. The interviews revealed broad understanding of the need for public debate in some scientific areas. Individual researchers do have ethical concerns and often recognise the need for assessments. At the same time, R&D institutions do not have the competencies (the know-how barrier) or the necessary credibility and independence (the independence barrier) to establish such a function themselves.

In terms of experimental activities, human and animal ethics are taken care of by well-established institutions. But when it comes to the consequences of the implementation of the research, the scientific community does not have access to assessment expertise. Such expertise may best be situated in existing institutions, using methods such as ethical accounting, ethical advising, technology and strategy analysis, or dialogue-based consensus processes. Establishing an assessment network and/or general education concerning assessment might also be useful.

Option 3: Assessment centres at universities

To ensure steady development of assessment capacity and expertise and local participation in assessments, universities could establish assessment centres in which both multi-disciplinary and more limited types of assessment could be practised and taught. The Technical University and Aalborg University have established such centres. Unstable funding, which forced the university to concentrate assessment expertise in one place, was one reason for establishing the centre at the Technical University. To some extent, such centres can in fact solve the unstable funding barrier.

If there is some permanent staff, the centres could in addition train experts from many disciplines of relevance to assessment activities. Thus, the centres need not necessarily focus only on technology or ethics, they could also focus on assessment methodology and practice. The establishment of such centres might have various motivations:

- The existence of a cross-disciplinary research council would motivate the shaping of cross-disciplinary expertise at the universities.
- Assessment and analysis of the consequences of R&D programmes would, by solving the unstable funding barrier, motivate assessment experts to stick to the field and thereby ensure a basis of expertise for the centres.
- Stronger strategic definition of R&D policy aims would clarify the need for multi-faceted assessments (social, ethical, environmental, etc.) and thus motivate experts and students from several disciplines to join the centres.

Option 4: Integration into university education

Ethics, philosophy, social values, and public attitudes as they relate to technology can made a part of university education. At Aalborg University, TA enters the education of engineers, and students' projects in order to be accepted must include assessments of the impacts on society.

In the long run, successful implementation of assessment education at universities will result in maximum integration of TA and ethics into the STI system. As one interviewee put it, "Integration has finally happened when TA is integrated into the brain."

Option 5: Regulations on the use of assessments

For public sector investments in new technology, assessments could be required by law in order to ensure that they are carried out. Such regulations would force decision-makers at all levels of the STI system to include assessments as part of the development of new technologies. By forcing assessments to be used more widely, motivation among assessors would rise, as would the credibility of the STI system, and the credibility of assessments in the public (the regulation problem). Further, the regulations would motivate a more strategic approach in the science policy system (the strategy barrier).

One obvious problem in this respect is the risk of establishing a new bureaucracy. This could be avoided by establishing an institution that would judge the need for assessments in order to avoid building up barriers for obviously uncomplicated technologies. The institution could use a set of relevance criteria.

VIII. INTERNATIONALISING THE STI SYSTEM

This chapter discusses the internationalisation of the STI system with specific reference to policies introduced to stimulate participation in international R&D programmes.

First, it reviews the main policy measures for internationalising the STI system. It treats the 1986 (PUF) initiative, the support to Danish experts working with the European Commission, the START programme (institutions of higher education and government research institutes), and the "Feasibility Study" (the business enterprise sector). Second, it discusses the actual internationalisation of the STI system, with specific attention given to EU programmes and the EUREKA programme.

Generally speaking, the policy for stimulating internationalisation has been a success. One indicator is the share of funding from abroad in total financing of R&D, which has doubled since 1985 both in the business enterprise sector and in the higher education sector and government research institutes. Little is known so far about how direct effects of participation in EU or EUREKA projects (patents, new products, etc.), for example, are transformed into new competencies and later into commercial or scientific competitiveness.

The chapter argues, on the basis of the interviews performed, that the policy measures for stimulating participation in international R&D programmes have been successful. However, attention needs to be paid to how the STI system moves through the different phases from participation in international R&D programmes to achievement of STI results, transformation into new competencies and later into commercial or scientific competitiveness. The international interviews conducted also reveal that the "general international competence" of Danish companies and institutions needs improvement in some areas in order to prepare them for further international integration.

Support for the internationalisation of the STI system and STI activities in general has had high policy priority in Denmark since the mid-1980s. Government appropriations for supporting participation in international R&D co-operation have increased from 1989 to 1994 by 31 per cent (or DKr 75 million). Most of the increase has gone to European space research at the European Space Agency (ESA), to nuclear research at the European Organization for Nuclear Research (CERN), and to participation in EUREKA.

At present, the Ministry of Research allocates approximately DKr 280 million annually for Danish participation in international R&D co-operation. The Danish Agency for Development of Trade and Industry allocates approximately DKr 140 million.

1. Organisational structure

Table VIII.1 presents Denmark's major international research efforts.

The European Union

R&D co-operation within the framework of the European Union is organised by four-year Framework Programmes, which are divided into sub-programmes. Approximately 80 per cent of the money spent in the Framework Programmes is devoted to contract research, for which the European Commission pays, on average, 50 per cent of total R&D costs. Co-ordination activities, demonstration projects, bursaries, subsidies, dissemination of R&D results, and the costs of the joint research facilities are supported as part of the EU Framework Programmes.

Influencing the decision-making process in the Framework Programmes is obviously very important for the EU member States. For purposes of clarity, the Danish system of influencing this process can be divided into two strands, although in reality, the two are very interrelated.

The first strand is related to the legal level of the decision-making process, and it is brought into play every time legal decisions are to be made by the EU Council of Ministers. The starting point might be a proposal for a Council decision put forward by

Table VIII.1. **Danish participation in international research collaboration**

	Number of members	Danish membership	Basis
EU – The European Union	12	1973	EC/Maastricht EURATOM treaty
EUREKA – European Initiative for high-technology research	20	1987	Declaration of intent
NATO – Science co-operation	16	1958	North Atlantic treaty
Nordic Council of Ministers co-operation	5	1971	Treaty
OECD – Organisation for Economic Co-operation and Development	24	1960	Treaty
CERN – European Organisation for Particle Research	19	1955	Treaty
ESA – European Space Agency	13	1973	Treaty
ESO – European Organisation for Astronomical Research	8	1967	Treaty
EMBL – European Molecular Biology Laboratory	15	1973	Treaty
ESRF – European Synchrotron Radiation Facility	12	1988	Treaty

Source: Ministry of Research.

the Commission, but often work will start even before that. Suggestions from national members of CREST or programme committees, on new programmes or third-country participation in certain programmes for example, can initiate the process as well.

Whether the starting point is a formal proposal by the Commission or rumours from the "early warning system", the Ministry for Research starts by drafting a first note on the proposal. The note is presented to the EU Special Committee on Science and Research, which consists of civil servants from all ministries and government agencies dealing with science and research. In each case, the EU committee then sees that every relevant ministry and government agency, as well as relevant national members of EU programme committees, comment on the proposal. When major proposals are concerned, relevant parts of the national science and research system (*e.g.* universities or government research institutes) are also consulted.

A concluding note, by the EU Special Committee on Science and Research, is then co-ordinated with Denmark's general EU policies by the EU committee served by the Ministry of Foreign Affairs. In principle, the EU committee then gives instructions for further negotiations to the research attachés of Denmark's permanent representation in Brussels. In practice, though, instructions are normally prepared by the Ministry of Research.

The second strand is related to the implementation of specific R&D programmes. A programme committee, with two representatives for each member State, advises the European Commission on the implementation of each R&D programme. In Denmark, a reference group is then established to support the national members of the programme committee and to disseminate knowledge about the programme activities to the national R&D system. Each reference group consists of approximately 12 members, and for the third Framework Programme, 15 such groups were established. Furthermore, a national programme administration is established for each programme. In principle, this adminis-tration is managed by the Ministry for Research, but in a number of cases, the national programme administration was delegated to another relevant ministry, such as the Minis-try of Industry. The reference groups and the national members of the programme committees are served by the Ministry of Research and in some instances, such as ESPRIT, by the Danish Agency for Development of Trade and Industry.

In January 1994, a number of task forces were formed in order to strengthen Danish impact on the content and implementation of the fourth Framework Programme. Each task force consists of from three to five members, including the Danish delegates to the EU programme committee in question. The task forces advise the Ministry of Research with respect to the preparation and implementation of specific EU programmes. They also prepare meetings of the programme committee, do follow-up work on decisions of the programme committee, take initiatives to strengthen Danish participation in the pro-gramme, and advise on how to inform potential Danish participants in the programme.

EUREKA – European Initiative for High-tech Research

EUREKA was founded in 1985 and is concerned with the competitiveness of individual companies. It is based on the bottom-up principle, whereby projects are launched on the basis of participants' views on the development of new products, processes, or systems. National project co-ordinators and a small EUREKA secretariat in Brussels then act as liaison with relevant international partners.

In Denmark, which joined the initiative in 1987, the role of national project co-ordination is managed by the Danish Agency for the Development of Industry and Trade. The Agency grants an annual DKr 60 million to companies and organisations participating in EUREKA projects, in the form of grant loans of up to 50 per cent of the project costs. In the event of commercial success, the loan has to be paid back.

At present, only about a dozen projects have begun to pay back loans, partly because the projects are not very mature and commercialisation of newly-developed products takes time, partly because EUREKA projects often are more costly than expected. Interviews indicate that EUREKA has become a definite part of the STI system. EUREKA's administration is somewhat isolated in the STI system, and political attention and economic resources are lagging behind the increase in the number of Danish participants. On average, Denmark spends less than other countries on EUREKA participation, yet it is doubtful whether further funds will be allocated to it.

Interviewees pointed out that it is difficult to get companies and universities to work together on EUREKA projects. Barriers for co-operation do not seem different from the barriers for industry-university co-operation in general, which are discussed in Chapter VI.

European scientific research facilities

Since the 1950s, European countries have joined forces in operational research co-operation. CERN and the European Synchrotron Radiation Facility (ESRF) involve accelerator facilities, the European Southern Observatory (ESO) has astronomical observatories, ESA engages in space research co-operation, and the European Molecular Biology Laboratory (EMBL) in co-operation in molecular biology. Danish research institutions and companies have contracts within ESA for a large number of projects in Earth observation, telecommunications, launcher rockets, the international space station (in co-operation with Russia and the United States), as well as research projects in astronomy, physics, biology, and physiology.

National responsibility for Danish participation in international research co-operation lies with the Ministry of Research. In this matter, the Ministry relies on advice from the research councils and the committees that have been set up in the various fields (the Danish Space Board, the Astronomical Committee, the Accelerator Committee, and the Synchrotron Radiation Committee). As an example of this advisory activity, the Danish Space Board has drawn up a strategy plan for 1993-97 which points to a number of areas (*e.g.* Earth observation for the monitoring of the environment) which should be given special priority, because Denmark is well-placed internationally in these fields.

Research policy co-operation

In parallel with its international co-operation in research activities, Denmark is involved in international co-operation on research policy under the auspices of the Nordic Council of Ministers, the OECD, and the United Nations.

With the formation of an independent Council of Ministers for Research and Education, work on research policy under the Nordic Council of Ministers has recently been given a new framework. The Council is expected to become a forum for consultative work and joint Nordic decision-making on European issues. One of the goals is to secure the best possible conditions for Nordic participation in capital-intensive international research programmes, for example through the formation of joint Nordic consortia. This approach has been applied for the Ocean Drilling Program (ODP) and the ESRF. With respect to the latter, Denmark has joined forces with the other Nordic countries in the NORDSYNC consortium to obtain as much influence as possible in the new facility in Grenoble.

The OECD does important work on the standardisation of data and statistics, so that R&D activities can be compared across the OECD countries. Partly on a Danish initiative, the OECD decided in 1992 to establish a Megascience Forum for the discussion of the optimal utilisation of existing and future megascience projects and programmes. So far, the Forum has held expert meetings on astronomy, deep drilling, global change research, oceanography, synchrotron radiation sources and neutron beams, and particle physics.

Co-operation in international organisations of the UN (*e.g.* UNESCO and WHO) and in the IMF also includes research policy topics.

Co-operation with Eastern Europe and developing countries

Danish support to Eastern Europe in the area of research and technology mainly takes the form of Nordic co-operation with specific countries, and participation in EU, EUREKA, and NATO programmes. At the Nordic level, there has been a desire to make a special effort in three Baltic countries. At the research policy level, this has so far resulted in a Danish-organised international evaluation of research in Latvia, and a corresponding Swedish effort in Estonia.

Within EUREKA, Denmark has supported expansion of the membership to Central and Eastern Europe; Hungary is now a member and Russia will shortly become one. EUREKA information offices are being established in other countries.

An increasing percentage of NATO's annual budgets for civil science will be used in the years ahead for research co-operation with the new partners of the North Atlantic Treaty from the former Warsaw Pact.

In 1993, more than DKr 25 million of Denmark's development assistance was spent on a special Research Assistance Programme, the aim of which is to improve the research capacity of the developing countries by strengthening co-operation between research institutions in Denmark and in the developing countries. The assistance is granted in particular to countries in Danish International Development Agency (DANIDA) programmes in the areas of agriculture, health, the natural sciences and the social sciences. Besides this, Denmark grants support to international institutions carrying out research on developing countries, primarily in the area of agriculture.

2. Policy measures

At the policy level, a number of initiatives designed to stimulate the internationalisation of the STI system have been implemented.

In 1986, the "PUF" Programme was founded to ensure that the Danish STI system would receive information on EU R&D programmes efficiently and rapidly. PUF was established as a joint initiative between the Ministry of Education, the Ministry of Industry, the Ministry of Foreign Affairs, and the Federation of Danish Industries. Practical co-operation is the responsibility of the Agency for Development of Trade and Industry and the present Ministry of Research. Its first role is to distribute information about EU programmes. The secretariat then assists in establishing contacts and gives general advice on how to apply for an EU research contract, legal aspects of the participation, etc. From 1993, the PUF secretariat extended its co-operation to the Innovation Unit of the Danish Technological Institute and became the Danish Value Relay Centre, supported by the EU Value Programme.

The START programme offers financial support for scientists from institutions of higher education and government research institutes who formulate applications for Research and Technological Development (RTD) contracts and plan joint RTD projects with foreign partners. It is administered by the national research councils, and government appropriations for the programme amount to DKr 8 million. Average grants for scientists are from DKr 50 000 to 200 000.

The "Feasibility Study" is a parallel programme oriented towards the business enterprise sector, and government appropriations amount to DKr 15 million. The programme is administered by the Danish Agency for Development of Trade and Industry.

In terms of more general policy measures for stimulating internationalisation, a programme oriented towards the creation of the Internal Market of the European Community was implemented in 1989-91. A total budget appropriation of DKr 95 million was administered by the Danish Agency for Development of Industry and Trade, which also represents Denmark in the Nordic Fund for Industrial Development.

In 1992, the Parliament passed an Act giving researchers from abroad the option of being taxed at 30 per cent rather than the normal tax rate, on the condition that they are employed on 6 to 36-month contracts in Denmark. Outstanding foreign personnel must receive salaries of over DKr 500 000 a year. The scheme makes it easier for Danish companies to attract key foreign personnel and foreign researchers to Denmark. For public sector research institutes, the scheme means better opportunities to involve outstanding international researchers in research projects and in the training of new researchers. When the scheme was introduced, it was estimated that it would apply to about 200 persons in the private sector and a similar number in the public sector. As of 1 June

1993, figures show that 505 persons have applied for the scheme; it is not possible to distinguish between researchers and other key personnel.

In order to strengthen R&D activities, especially in the research-intensive, export-oriented parts of Danish industry, and to increase incentives for companies to participate in international research programmes, 125 per cent tax allowances are granted for costs incurred in connection with participation in international research projects. The scheme covers participation in EUREKA research projects, in programmes under the auspices of the Nordic Industrial Foundation, and in programmes under the EU Framework Programme. This research support is estimated to amount to approximately DKr 35 million a year. The rules restrict support to projects approved before the end of 1993.

Finally, DANVIS, a programme for visiting scientists, was launched in 1993. It is a five-year, cross-disciplinary programme administered by the Danish Research Academy which aims to further the internationalisation and quality of Danish research communities, increase the level of co-operation in research with countries such as the United States and Japan, and procure more active exchanges of scientists between countries. The visiting scientists are to participate actively in the Danish research education communities and in research education. They receive a salary that should attract highly-qualified scientists, and the primary criterion for funding is the qualification of the individual scientist.

The programme was motivated by research evaluations in health and agriculture, which revealed an urgent need to internationalise the Danish research communities. There also appeared a need to exploit international research resources more effectively.

Interviews stress the DANVIS programme and the tax-reduction act as measures that have had an important effect on the ability to attract highly-qualified scientists from abroad, and support Danish scientists who go abroad. In the case of one government research establishment, the possibilities opened up by the tax-reduction act have made it possible to buy attractive apartments to house visiting scientists.

On the negative side, interviews brought out the fragmentation and lack of co-ordination in support for internationalisation of the STI system. Some schemes support participation in EU RTD programmes using slightly different priorities and criteria than those for EUREKA projects. Companies and institutions interviewed noted a lack of co-ordination, for example, when EU RTD projects led to near-market R&D projects, which naturally fit within the framework of EUREKA. Competencies developed in EU or EUREKA projects might be developed in areas of national interest, but again, slightly different priorities and criteria apply for strategic programmes such as FØTEK and BIOTEK. Thus, coherence and interaction among schemes and programmes need to be improved so as to support the entire chain from participation in international R&D programmes, achievement of STI results, transformation into new competencies and later into commercial or scientific competitiveness.

3. Actual internationalisation

Viewed from outside, the Danish STI system is already highly internationalised. According to interviews with British, French, and German companies and institutions that have co-operated with Danish companies and institutions in R&D projects, Danes possess most of the qualifications needed for good international performance. As Chapter I indicated, performing well in international R&D co-operation is a necessity for the survival of the Danish STI system. Below, a presentation of the cultural characteristic of Danes in international STI co-operation will follow a review of experience gained from recent studies on the impact of EU RTD programmes and EUREKA projects.

EU RTD programmes

Danish participation in EU RTD programmes increased considerably during the late 1980s in a number of ways. First, the number of participants has increased, partly due to the fact that the programmes themselves have increased in number. The diversity of participants has also increased. Today, participants include large companies as well as small and medium-sized enterprises, and universities and government research institutes as well as independent R&D institutes.

Table VIII.2 presents two very simple indicators of the impact of participation in EU research projects: the extent to which R&D employment has risen as a result of the R&D contract; and the extent to which economic resources, originally devoted to the R&D work and then replaced in part by EU allocations, have been used for new R&D projects. It indicates that in 65 per cent of projects, obtaining an EU RTD contract led to an increase in R&D personnel.

Table VIII.3 shows the overall impact of EU RTD contracts. New research-based knowledge is the main impact, followed by increased skills among R&D personnel; education of new/young researchers rates relatively low.

In terms of industrial competitiveness, participation in EU RTD programmes primarily affects the output of new products and processes and the time lag between participation and actual output. Table VIII.4 shows a rather short time lag between participation

Table VIII.2. **Contractors**
**Impact of R&D-contract: more R&D personnel
and alternative use of allocated economic resources**

(percentages)

Personnel/economic resources	Company contractors	University contractors	Total
More R&D-personnel employed	60	68	65
Economic resources allocated to new R&D projects	10	19	16

Source: EC Commission 1994.

Table VIII.3. **Contractors**
Overall impact of European Union R&D contract

(percentages)

Impact	Company contractors	University contractors	Total
New research-based knowledge	36	37	36
Increased skills of R&D personnel	17	19	19
Education of new/young researchers	8	12	11
Better links to other R&D-units	19	14	16
Start of external R&D co-operation	17	15	15
Other	3	3	3
Total	100	100	100

Source: EC Commission 1994.

Table VIII.4. **Contractors**
Impact on new products and processes
All contractors

(percentages)

Expected impact – time lag	0-3 years	3-5 years	More than 5 years	Total
Products	45	35	20	100
Processes	46	35	19	100
Total	46	34	20	100

Source: EC Commission 1994.

and actual output in the form of new products or processes; 46 per cent of all respondents expect new products and/or processes within three years and 80 per cent within five years. (This is an average for projects terminated some years ago as well as for ongoing projects.) Table VIII.5 indicates the number of projects expected to result in new products (300), processes (169), standards (93), or patents (77) as a specific outcome of participation in EU RTD programmes. Projects that neither generate or expect to generate new products, processes, or patents may often be more oriented towards social research and technology or basic research.

Table VIII.6 indicates where contractors obtain supplementary R&D financing. In 1986, a similar study showed that 52 per cent came from the organisations' own resources (Møller, 1987). The share has increased to 63 per cent overall, and to 86 per cent in private companies. Interviewees indicated that economic support from other national or regional sources is often allocated for a specific and limited part of a larger

123

Table VIII.5. **Contractors**
Specific outputs in form of new products, processes, patents or standards
Actual or expected numbers

Output	ESPRIT	BREU	RILB	STEP	SLC/2	Other	Total
New Products	37	19	20	4	7	113	300
New Processes	28	22	19	6	5	89	169
Patents	11	12	13	3	2	36	77
Standards	17	7	15	8	3	43	93

Source: EC Commission 1994.

R&D programme of which the EU contract is a part. Larger projects require greater co-financing and may prevent some SMEs and small university institutes from participating.

The European Commission's 1994 survey confirms this tendency. Large EU RTD programmes generally have larger individual projects, and they tend to favour large companies and institutions. Such a situation seems to produce fewer tangible results than those produced by small and medium-sized contractors in small and medium-sized projects.

The experts interviewed do not generally use the exploratory studies conducted or ordered by the EU while advising on preparation of national programmes. These have to focus on national R&D specialisations in order to support the strongest national R&D fields. If there is an EU RTD programme in the same field (as is very often the case), complementary themes are proposed.

However, complementarity often turns to supplementarity in the administration of national RTD programmes. According to national RTD managers, a RTD project is favoured if national support will enable the project to obtain EU support as well. EU

Table VIII.6. **Contractors**
Sources of supplementary R&D financing

(percentages)

Sources	Company	University	Total
Other national or regional schemes	12	21	17
Basic funding	0	16	16
Private sources	2	9	7
Own sources	86	54	63
Total	100	100	100

Source: EC Commission 1994.

support offers a strong argument for national support, but this is only possible if EU and national RTD programmes are very closely related.

National experts generally benefit from exchanging views on RTD trends with experts from other countries in the sense that their views on international trends are reinforced if and when other experts confirm these views. They can then give better and more reliable advice on the strong points of the national RTD infrastructure and possibilities for further improvement. At the same time, exchanging views with international experts and agreeing on international trends is useful when defining fields in which R&D investments can or should be avoided since other countries are expected to make them. Such discussions take place whenever experts meet, *e.g.* in advisory functions to the European Commission or in specific fora.

In advising the Commission on setting up programmes, on the other hand, experts do not generally consider the equivalent national programmes. It is felt that activities at the EU level should not be influenced by specific national interests but should reflect only EU interests. Danish experts do not see themselves as representing Danish interests in such circumstances, and they seldom have a political mandate.

Of course, EU or simply common interests are often hard to define, and what is seen as an important issue in one country may be neglected in others. To some extent, the views of small and large countries diverge. In large countries, so it is said, experts from university institutions prefer to let their large national companies define the national interest for specific programmes, so that programmes recommended by experts from large countries tend to subsidise large company R&D budgets rather than take an objective view of the strengths/weaknesses of national or EU RTD infrastructures. For example, Denmark only supported the JESSIE programme to show its general goodwill towards EU RTD co-operation. There also appears to be a difference between northern and southern European countries. Northern experts are more oriented towards research itself and tend to place quality above relevance, while southern experts are more oriented toward practical use and demonstration.

Experts generally emphasize that the EU RTD programmes have clearly improved the level and content of EU RTD co-operation as well as the co-operation between companies and universities. This is particularly true for agricultural research, an area in which Danish universities and government R&D institutes have strongly increased industrial co-operation during the past decade, first in the context of EU RTD programmes (often with international industry partners) and second, in co-operative efforts with national industry.

Increased international co-operation has definitely improved the quality of Danish research and the internationalisation of younger researchers. Administrators and policy-makers highlight the internationalisation of PhD students through participation in EU RTD work.

Experts also point to the impact of EU RTD programmes in fields facing dramatic changes. Agriculture is one example: if EU agricultural policy collapses, all agriculturally-important countries will face huge problems in applying biotechnological alternatives, RTD and no single country will be able to effect the transition alone. This may prohibit both the implementation of the necessary RTD work and the actual investment in new production.

Experts finally emphasize the importance of EU RTD programmes in fields where, for different reasons, national RTD policies discourage investment. In such fields, EU RTD programmes may be the only source of survival for researchers and R&D units. Administrators and policy-makers point to the environment as an areas where EU RTD programmes play an important role in giving somewhat neglected areas of research more policy attention. The humanities and the social sciences are generally not a focal point of national RTD policy-making, but they are integrated into RTD policy-making for the Environment Programme. The fourth Framework Programme also gives increased attention to the humanities.

EUREKA co-operation

Danish companies and institutions participate in more than 100 out of 800 current EUREKA projects. Danish SMEs participate in one-third of all EUREKA projects in which Denmark participates. The high rate of participation indicates that EUREKA co-operation is well suited to the Danish business enterprise sector, its industrial structure, and the needs and competencies of its companies and institutions.

In a study of 28 Danish companies and six technological service institutes participating in EUREKA projects, the principal benefits identified were the renewal of scientific equipment and improvement of scientific work processes and methods, linkages to new trading and co-operation partners, inspiration for new strategies, and more generally a higher "high technology corporate image" (Kreiner, 1993).

Danes in international STI co-operation

Presenting Danish cultural characteristics is no easy task, and there is always the risk of oversimplification and error. However, interviews with companies and institutions in France, Germany, and the United Kingdom that have experience in working with Danish companies and institutions in STI projects pinpoint important common cultural characteristics – both strengths and weaknesses – with respect to their professional competencies, their human qualities, and their international orientation.

In terms of their *professional competencies*, Danes are viewed as serious, qualified, thorough, and very professional experts within their fields (specific knowledge). They are good at planning and co-ordinating projects and plan very thoroughly, taking all details into account and trying to avoid conflicts and problems.

On the negative side, the Danes are sometimes very slow to reach a decision and act on it, given their tendency to analyse every detail. Sometimes such thorough preparation is unnecessary. Danish partners could be more pragmatic and should try to isolate specific relevant areas for analysis.

While most respondents thought that their Danish partners showed flexibility and willingness and ability to adjust project planning when necessary, some Danish partners in some projects showed a tendency towards inflexibility. In such cases, the Danes, who had put great effort into planning, refused to deviate from the project plans once they had been accepted by all parties, even though new possibilities arose in the course of the project, and it would have been fruitful to adjust the plans.

In terms of their *human qualities*, Danes are seen as very pleasant and relaxed – easy people to work with. All the respondents described the Danes as having a very direct, open relationship with those around them; they treated everybody equally, they were not formal and did not "categorise" people. The social aspect of an international R&D partnership is as important as the specific disciplinary competencies of each partner, and the Danes are perceived as caring about creating a positive atmosphere of mutual interest and trust. The Danes are very polite, considerate people, who try to make sure that everything goes well.

They did not "show off" but had a natural relationship to their own strengths. The respondents re-emphasized the high quality of the Danes' competencies and expert knowledge, their professionalism. They also described the Danes as trustworthy people who kept their promises, and only promised what they knew they could live up to.

On the other hand, some respondents felt that Danes tried above all to avoid controversy. On the face of it, this is not negative behaviour, but it is still necessary to be able to cope with and handle the conflicts and disagreements that inevitably arise in projects involving several partners with different cultural and professional backgrounds. Some respondents noted that, if controversies arose, the Danes avoided bringing them out into the open. In one case, the Danish partner withheld important information in order to try and avoid conflict. The Danes were also described as reserved, not showing emotions and feelings as much as others.

In terms of their *international orientation*, it was clear that Danes are very experienced in international co-operation, and they are in many respects internationally-oriented. They know foreign languages, especially English, and they are used to working in an international environment. Most respondents felt that the Danes seemed to have a good relationship with the EU authorities and succeeded in obtaining the EU R&D projects they wanted, by lobbying and participating in relevant negotiations, committees, etc.

Moreover, a couple of respondents noted that, despite its small size, when compared with the large EU countries, Denmark always had strong opinions and held fast to them. One respondent pointed out that Danish companies do not have the same scepticism towards the European Union as the "man on the street" (as expressed by the Danish "no" to the Maastricht treaty). Danes who do business and collaborate in other ways with international partners have a very positive view of the EU.

However, the Danes can also sometimes be rather ethnocentric. At certain times, they display a "Nordic arrogance", thinking that everything Scandinavian is best. Another respondent remarked that a consequence of the Danes' strong belief in their own strengths is that they are blind to the strengths of other countries; for example, because of their very high qualifications within the fields of environmental research/protection, they may forget that other countries also have advanced competencies in this area.

Some international partners also complained that the Danes did not show much consideration or understanding for problems their partners have at home, concerning patent regulations, for example.

Given that Danish companies and institutions are to work even more on international STI projects in the years to come, it is important to consider whether or not specific initiatives can be taken to improve on the weaknesses mentioned above.

LIST OF INTERVIEWS

National interviews: Policy level

Mr. Arne Skov Andersen,
Consultant
The Economic Council of the Labour
Movement

Mr. Christian Buhl,
General Manager
Chairman of the Industry and Trade
Development Council's ATSI-committee
Danish Agency for Development of Trade
Industry and Trade

Mr. Niels E. Busch,
former General Manager of Danish Technological Institute

Professor Bent Christensen
University of Copenhagen

Mr. Jan Daub,
Civil Engineer
Danish Energy Agency

Mr. Ole Fejerskov,
Rectoraqfl The Danish Research Academy

Mr. Mogens Granborg,
General Manager
Former Chairman of the Industry and
Trade Development
Danisco Ltd.

Mr. Per Grønborg,
Department Director

The Technical Research Council
Ministry of Research

Mr. Anders Frølund,
Head of Section
The Environmental Research Programme
Science Park Aarhus

Mr. Niels Juul Jensen,
Assistant Director
National Agency of Environmental
Protection

Mr. Hans Peter Jensen,
Rector
Chairman of the Rector's Conference
The Technical University of Denmark

Mr. Lars Bernhard Jørgensen,
Deputy Permanent Secretary
Department of the Ministry of Industry

Mr. Bent Kiemer,
General Manager
The Danish Fund for Industrial Growth

Mr. Poul Knudsen,
Special Consultant
National project Co-ordinator, EUREKA
Danish Agency for Development
of Industry and Trade

Mr. Mogens Kring,
General Manager
Danish Agency for Development
of Industry and Trade

Mr. Peder Olesen Larsen,
General Manager
The Danish National Research Foundation

Professor Poul Christian Matthiessen
Chairman of the Carlsberg Foundation

Ms Vibeke Hein Olsen,
Head of Division
Ministry of Research

Mr. Jan Plovsing,
General Manager
Chairman in the Assembly of Directors
of Government Research Establishments
National Institute of Social Research

Mr. Erik B. Rasmussen,
General Manager
Executive Director in the Danish
Academy of Technical Sciences
Chairman of the Board in the Danish
Development Finance Corporation Ltd.

Mr. Torben Kornbech Rasmussen,
Deputy Permanent Secretary
Ministry of Education

Mr. Curt Sander,
General Manager
Chairman in the Co-ordination Committee
for the PIFT-programme
Danish Agency for Development
of Industry and Trade

Mr. Ib Skovgaard,
Deputy Permanent Secretary
Danish Farmers Union

Ms Eva Steiness,
Chairwoman in the Danish Council
for Research Policy
Ministry of Research

Mr. Lars Stigel,
Head of Secretariat
The Environmental Research Programme
Science Park Aarhus

Ms Inge Thygesen,
Permanent Secretary
Ministry of Education

Ms Vibeke Zeuthen,
Assistant Head of Academy
Danish Academy of Technical Sciences

Professor Knud Østergaard
Chairman of the Danish Research
Councils' Chairman College
The Technical University of Denmark

Performance level

Ms Jytte Mollerup Andersen,
Head of Department
Danisco Ltd.

Ms Søren Stougaard Dalby,
Director of Research
Grundfos Ltd.

Mr. Poul Dyhr-Mikkelsen,
Director of Technology
Danfoss Ltd.

Mr. Torben Grønning,
General Manager
DELTA

Mr. Niels Hansen,
Deputy Permanent Secretary
Risø National Laboratory

Mr. Arne Bækgaard Hansen,
Civil Engineer
Danish Meat Research Institute

Mr. Jens Morten Hansen,
Deputy Director
Geological Survey of Denmark

Mr. Ejler Lautrup Holm,
Assistant Director
Aalborg Ciserv International Ltd.

Mr. Jørgen Honoré,
acting Executive Director
Danish Technological Institute

Mr. Thorvald Kjær,
Planner
Danfoss Ltd.

Mr. Bent Koch,
Head of Division
FORCE-Institutes

Mr. N. Elers Koch,
General Manager
Danish Forest and Landscape Research Institute

Mr. Hans Jørgen Larsen,
General Manager
Danish Building Research Institute

Mr. Tom Lautrup-Petersen,
acting Dean
University of Aarhus

Mr. K.B. Madsen,
General Manager
Danish Meat Research Institute

Ms Inge Mærkedahl,
Assistant Director
National Institute of Social Research

Mr. Kjeld Møllgård,
Rector
University of Copenhagen

Mr. A. Hjortshøj Nielsen,
General Manager
Biotechnological Institute

Mr. Lars Chr. Nielsen,
General Manager
Biotechnological Institute

Mr. Eigil Steen Pedersen,
Executive Director
COWI-Consult Ltd.

Research Professor Peter Roepstorff
University of Odense

Mr. Henrik Sandbech,
General Manager
Danish Environmental Research Institute

Mr. Torben Sørensen,
General Manager
Danish Hydraulic Institute

Mr. Niels Vejgaard-Nielsen,
Head of Division
DELTA

Mr. Peter Vesterdorf,
Associate Professor
University of Aarhus

International interviews

Norway

Mr. Hans Skoie,
Deputy Permanent Secretary
Institute of Research and Academic Education

Mr. Arild Underdal,
Deputy Rector
University of Oslo

Mr. Bjarne Waaler,
Deputy Rector
University of Oslo

Mr. Leif Westgaard,
Deputy Permanent Secretary
Research Council of Norway

Ms. Kari Balke Øiseth,
Adviser
The Royal Ministry of Education, Research and Church Affairs

The Netherlands

Mr. Emil Broesterhuizen
Head, Natural
and Engineering Science Division
Ministry of Education and Science

Ms. Bea J. Hoogheid
Deputy Head,
International Technology Policy
Ministry of Economic Affairs

Mr. N. van Hulst,
Deputy Permanent Secretary
Ministry of Economic Affairs

Mr. Koen de Pater
Head,
International Technology Policy
Ministry of Economic Affairs

Mr. Hans P.M. Sterk,
Deputy Permanent Secretary
Ministry of Economic Affairs

Ms. Margot van Vliet,
Head of Section
Ministry of Economic Affairs

Sweden

Mr. Nils Karlson,
Political Adviser
Ministry of Education

Mr. Sven Sjögren,
Assistant Under-Secretary
Ministry of Industry and Commerce

Mr. Lennart Stenberg,
Programme Director
The Swedish National Board for Industrial
and Technical Development (NUTEK)

United Kingdom

Mr. Rupert Huxter
Head of Team,
International Affairs
Office of Science and Technology

Mr. Martin Marcus
Head of Team, Higher Education
Department of Education

Mr. Lewis Read,
Head of Section
LINK Secretariat
Government Offices

Dr. R.K. Bolingbroke
Alcan International Ltd.
Banbury Laboratory

Mr. D.M. Colwilll,
Senior Project Manager
Transport Research Laboratory

Dr. S. Elliot
University of Southhampton

Dr. Alan Maries
Head,
Construction Materials Department
Trafalgar House Technology

Prof. Bernhard de Neumann
City University

Mr. Gary Raw
Head,
Human Factors and Health Section
Building Research Establishment

France

Prof. Marcel Cheyrezy
Bouygues SA

Mr. G. Pavic
Head of Section
Centre Technique
des Industries Mécaniques

Mr. G. Pilot
Assistant Director International
Laboratoire Central des Ponts
et Chaussées

Germany

Mr. Holger Herbrig
Head, Networks
SEL Research Centre

Prof. Felix Rauer
University of Bremen

Dr. Martin-Cristoph Wanner
Frauenhofer IPA

Mr. Frank Weinhold,
PhD-student
Max Planck Institut für Chemie

Mr. Dieter Wybranietz
Head of Software Department
Telenorma GmbH Bosch Telecom

EXAMINERS' REPORT

PREFACE

This document constitutes the Examiners' Report.

The examining team included:

- Ms. Agnes Aylward, Director, Department of Tourism and Trade, Ireland.
- Prof. Chris Freeman, Em. Professor, Science Policy Research Unit, University of Sussex, United Kingdom.
- Mr. Kaj Linden, Senior Vice-President, Nokia Corporation, Finland.
- Sir Peter Swinnerton-Dyer, Professor, Department of Pure Mathematics and Mathematical Studies, University of Cambridge, United Kingdom.

The review team were assisted by J.E. Aubert (Rapporteur) and H. Mieras of the OECD Secretariat.

This report relies on the Background Report furnished by the Danish authorities and on the information gathered by the team of examiners during their visits to Denmark on 1-4 June and 19-20 September 1994. The examiners and the Secretariat of the OECD wish to thank the Danish authorities, and, in particular, the Ministry of Research which requested and co-ordinated the study, for the excellent organisation and the remarkable hospitality that they received and which greatly aided them in their work. They appreciated the support given to the study by the Danish Agency for Development of Trade and Industry which co-commissioned it, and the Ministry of Education which was associated to it. They also express their gratitude to the representatives of the various communities whom they encountered – academics, scientists, technologists, industrialists, trade unionists, etc. – who spoke freely about the problems of the Danish research and innovation system.

The review team wish to emphasize, however, that despite the merits of the analyses and information that were furnished to them, the report suffers from the limitations inherent in the exercise itself, which, by its very nature and given the time allowed to it, cannot treat all the relevant questions fully and in depth.

In light of this, they sought to concentrate on the problems that appeared most urgent, at a time when the Danish research and innovation policies are undergoing reorganisation. They hoped to make a contribution to the discussions surrounding this process, in as objective and neutral a manner as possible, in the form of international expertise drawing upon the experience of the Member countries of the OECD.

The opinions expressed in this report are those of the review team, and they do not necessarily reflect those of the OECD and its Member countries.

The draft report was discussed at the final review meeting, held in Copenhagen on 31 October 1994. This final version includes a few changes in the text made as a result of those discussions. A brief summary account of the meeting is attached in Appendix.

MAIN RECOMMENDATIONS

On the whole the Danish science, technology and innovation (STI) system has evolved favourably since the last OECD review in 1987. However a number of actions are needed to improve its management and performance:

1. The R&D effort is at the core of the STI system, even though R&D is not synonymous with scientific and innovative activity. In an increasingly knowledge-intensive economy, a sustained R&D effort is necessary to creation of employment in the longer term and to supporting Danish efforts to enlarge its share of world-class research. The Government's target of reaching 2 per cent of GNP by the year 2000 should be therefore maintained, and state allocations needed to achieve this goal should be guaranteed.

2. Public support to R&D should be better focused and co-ordinated. To this end, a national R&D strategy should be established and implemented, so as to provide a clear, medium-term framework for all concerned actors. Related to a clear view of the country's technological and economic development, this strategy should define national goals, key R&D areas for priority support and related major programmes and actions.

3. The responsibility for defining the R&D strategy and annual preparation and monitoring of the corresponding R&D budget should be given to a Ministry of Research with adequate administrative and financial power. The new Ministry of Research should be given the responsibility and power to efficiently fulfil an overall co-ordinating function for all public sector R&D and support to industrial R&D.

4. The Ministry should be assisted in this task by appropriate advisory mechanisms. In this respect we recommend that the two-tier structure of advisory councils be consolidated, with a clear separation between the "macro" policy-making level and the "sectoral" level involved in grant administration. The role of the Research Policy Council is to advise on the overall research policy, its priorities and issues in relation to the country's needs and capabilities. The main research councils, operating in their specific scientific fields of competence, should be concerned with informing the Government on related issues and with administering grant allocations.

5. The Government should support academic and public research more selectively, with support going to strategic research that can lead to wealth creation and be

exploited by local industry, to groups with good track records, and to individuals rated as outstanding by international standards. We commend the establishment of the National Foundation for Basic Research, which does work that cannot be easily divided among the individual research councils and which seems in a better position than the latter to provide the financial support necessary for scientific endeavours of international calibre.

6. Evaluations of strategic programmes and scientific fields of national interest should be continued and expanded, under the supervision of the ministry in charge of research. They can help make it possible to identify the strongest teams and institutions, eliminate weaker ones, and rationalise an R&D grant system which seems complex and has many sources of funding. Policy conclusions from these evaluations should be implemented.

7. Concerning the universities, we commend the recent law giving them more autonomy and strengthening the management capability of the rector's office and of representatives of the faculty. We are concerned about university financing and more particularly with the regulations that make grant funding for teaching dependent on the number of students who successfully pass their final examinations: this will create pressure to lower the pass/fail borderline.

8. We are also concerned about the financing of university research: it would be advisable that all institutions/departments that seek to maintain international standards divide the government allocation equally between education and research. Industry funding of university research seems excessively low and should be increased, possibly with appropriate tax incentives.

9. As regards public sector R&D institutes, continued efforts need to be made to improve their efficiency and ability to respond to the needs of the Danish economy. It is, in general, not advisable to remove the responsibility for government research institutes from their sponsoring ministries; however, it is a good thing that the ministry responsible for research has been explicitly given a role to play in determining their budgets, programmes, and evaluations.

10. The approved technical services institutes (ATSIs) play a vital function in the dissemination of technology; we feel that the core grant to ATSIs has dropped too low and recommend that an increase be considered. We also recommend that the problem of access to their services, notably for smaller firms, be dealt with.

11. In view of the importance of small firms in the Danish economy, we suggest that the government increase its efforts to stimulate their creation and growth by providing an appropriate environment in terms of availability of capital, quality of management training, adequate support services such as science parks, facilities for access to international networks and sources of funds (e.g. from the European Union), etc.

12. More generally, the national R&D and innovation effort will bear fruit all the more readily if the right framework conditions exist in the economy as a whole – in terms of financial and tax systems, development of human resources, trade and competition regulations, communication infrastructures, etc. In this respect, we were favourably impressed by the ''resource areas'' exercise launched by

the Industry and Trade Development Council, which helps identify growth areas in manufacturing and services and focus attempts at innovation. While this strategic effort should not lead to supporting R&D in specific industrial sectors, we believe that the bodies involved in R&D policy-making (*e.g.* national research councils) could usefully be associated with these exercises.

13. We suggest paying more attention to the development of information technology infrastructures and services, which will be called on to play a key role in the future development of all economies. The fact that the new Ministry of Research now has telecommunications and IT policy among its responsibilities offers a good opportunity to develop an appropriate strategy in these areas.

14. To sum up, we think that science, technology and innovation policies in Denmark need more strategic vision, rigour and firmness in their management. This does not necessarily mean that reshuffling or radical change is required.

I. INTRODUCTION

1. The context of the review

Denmark's economic situation is marked by contrasts. It has succeeded in eliminating most of the macroeconomic disequilibria it suffered from in the 1980s. Inflation is moderate, the trade balance is positive, and the public finances have been put in order. One dark spot remains, however: unemployment. Unemployment affects 12 per cent of the working population, a figure slightly higher than the average in the European Union (11.6 per cent) and considerably higher than the OECD area average (8.3 per cent). This is a source of concern, as there has been a constant rise in unemployment for some 15 years, with very little response to improvements in the economic situation.

Reducing unemployment depends on many factors, both social and economic, as already noted in the recent OECD Economic Survey of Denmark,[1] which particularly emphasised the measures relating to the labour market. This review deals with science and technology policy, which has the potential to stimulate innovation and to create and maintain employment. Science and technology can help strengthen and broaden the industrial production base, maintain competitiveness in manufacturing and stimulate new activities, especially in services; but its effects are usually medium-term rather than short-term. Today, the industries that are creating employment are the knowledge-intensive ones, including high-technology sectors.

This is why the Government, in response to demands from Parliament, proposed to pursue a strong R&D effort – to reach 2.0 per cent of GDP in the year 2000 against 1.7 per cent today – which followed on the already remarkable effort that has been made for several years, particularly by industry. The intention of expanding the powers of the Ministry of Research in the new Government formed after the September 1994 elections is also a step in the right direction.

Increased expenditure on R&D is not, in itself, enough. Research must find applications in technology, and technology must be translated into new processes and products that are perfected and disseminated throughout the economy. In other words, innovation is also necessary, and it does not follow, directly and automatically, from research. Indeed, improving the path from research to innovation is a major problem for all European countries. There must be a favourable climate in which many factors work together: entrepreneurs, qualified human resources at all levels in firms, a legal, fiscal and institutional framework that stimulates and protects creativity, effective transportation and communication infrastructures, etc. The public authorities are aware of this: for instance, substantial reforms have been implemented to maintain the high-quality educational system that has been one of the bases of Danish prosperity; thought is being given to measures for better exploiting areas of growth and employment possibilities throughout the economy.

The very fact that the Government requested this review by the OECD is further confirmation of the seriousness with which it addresses the issues. Seven years have passed since the last review, and the present one makes it possible to measure the changes made and the efforts undertaken in the conduct of research and innovation policy.

2. Changes since the 1987 review

While recognising the strengths of the Danish scientific and technical system and its general soundness, the 1987 review[2] identified a certain number of problems that required vigorous measures on the part of government. Some of these problems persist, others have faded, and new problems have, to a certain extent, appeared. These points are clearly identified in the Background Report submitted by the Danish authorities for the current review. We will limit ourselves here to a few essential points.

Among the persistent problems, one for which a satisfactory solution should be found quickly, is the need to establish an efficient and effective structure for science and technology policy institutions. Difficulties remain at different levels. At the ministerial level, where policy is made, efficient structures with substantial means have not been set up, despite the creation (early 1993) of a Ministry of Research and Technology, later restricted to a Ministry of Research. At the level of policy orientation, the establishment of a Research Policy Council (as the 1987 review had suggested) has not had all the expected beneficial effects and has been accompanied by rivalries with the existing sectoral research councils and by frictions with the Ministry. At the level of financing, the large number of public R&D funding sources, which the 1987 report found surprising, seems scarcely to have diminished, since there would be still more than 60. This state of affairs, which is difficult to change, finds its roots in the very foundations of Danish society, which constantly seeks consensus and is concerned about egalitarian distribution among all its members. This inevitably has repercussions: principal among them are the lack of strategic focus and the scattering of resources over large numbers of activities of sub-critical size.

Among the problems that have diminished and that were of concern to the 1987 examiners should be mentioned the positive changes that have occurred in the management of the educational system. The reforms implemented in the wake of the 1992 University Law have improved the balance of power in the management of universities. The universities had found themselves managed by two authorities, the one traditionally responsible for their administration (the Rector's Office) and the other made of representatives of "non-teaching" groups, notably students. This situation was detrimental to the proper functioning of the universities. The 1992 law re-established the principle of a single responsible authority with what appear to be very positive results. At the same time the management of universities has become more independent of the central authorities.

Finally, the "University in growth" plan, announced in August 1994, indicates the Government's intention to ensure a substantial increase in the budgetary allocations to higher education institutions over the long term. This would usefully reduce the constraints that have resulted in particular from the large increases in numbers of students in the past several years.

Among the new problems that have arisen may be mentioned certain tensions surrounding the structure of technological services, a key point for technology diffusion in the economy and a topic on which the 1987 report was full of praise. This structure has tended to break up into many separate bodies. Reforms that would impose mergers were necessary, but certain restructurings have also created difficulties. Further, "fixed" institutional funding has been considerably reduced, so that institutes have been obliged to finance a very large share of their activities by contracts with firms, on market terms. The large share of variable resources affects the conditions under which services are rendered and, in particular, makes it difficult for small enterprises to use them. Yet small firms constitute a very large share of the Danish economic fabric.

3. Objectives and plan of the report

The Examiners' Report, as is customary, seeks to address the issues that appear the most important by offering possibilities for solutions. Its goal is to offer food for thought to nourish the discussion of reforms, which is generally already under way, so that, after as full a debate as possible, a consensus on the most appropriate reforms will emerge.

In our report, we have not tried to exhaustively cover science, technology and innovation policies and the many issues involved. We have attempted to focus on what we feel are the most crucial problems. First, we discuss strategic issues of national importance related to the research and innovation effort and insist on the need for a better focus (Chapter II). We then devote a chapter to examining the institutional framework in which R&D policy is designed, implemented, and evaluated, and we provide suggestions for ministries' responsibilities, advisory bodies, and funding mechanisms (Chapter III). We then deal with the university sector, mostly in terms of its research activities, leaving teaching and education issues aside when they are not directly connected to research (Chapter IV). Public sector activities are then examined under two headings: the government research institutes and the approved technical services institutes (Chapter V). Finally, we address means of boosting R&D and innovation in the business sector, discussing issues such as availability of finance, management skills, etc. (Chapter VI).

In order to complement the summary presented at the beginning of this report, *we highlight our recommendations (in italics) throughout the text.*

II. STRATEGIC ISSUES

As noted in Chapter I, Denmark's high unemployment rate remains a persistent and worrisome problem, despite the elimination of most major macroeconomic imbalances. In the discussions we had during our visit, the unemployment problem was often linked with concerns about Denmark's competitive position and new international challenges. Competition from countries with lower wages, especially in Eastern Europe, was often mentioned as a threat to Danish exports. The people we talked to seemed generally to agree that increasing the knowledge content and quality of Danish products is the only feasible way to solve the problem. However, it should be clear that R&D and high technology cannot solve structural problems in a society where there is an oversupply of workers adapted to older industries and an undersupply of workers with special skills for new industries. S&T cannot create jobs for persons graduating from high schools or universities in fields where unemployment is already high.

Whatever the contribution of science and technology to economic and social development, two important elements of a S&T-based strategy are, first, to strengthen the R&D system and improve its efficiency and, second, to improve the interrelations between R&D and industrial innovation. Finally, there is a need to focus appropriately the efforts made in these respects.

1. The national R&D effort

We found general agreement on the need to increase national investment in science and technology, a need clearly reflected in the Prime Minister's statement that expenditures on R&D should reach 2.0 per cent of GNP in the year 2000. The same target (2.0 per cent in 2000) was formulated in 1987 when the last OECD review was held.

Danish R&D expenditure has increased considerably since this target was first formulated. This recent increase is mainly attributable to the business sector; industrial R&D expenditures almost doubled in the period 1985-91, a better result than that of most OECD countries. As a percentage of GDP, business R&D rose from 0.69 per cent in 1985 to 0.99 per cent in 1991. Public R&D, instead, increased only slightly over this period. This means that, in order to reach this target, public R&D expenditures will also have to increase considerably. Moreover, it must be remembered that wealth creation from public R&D is much harder than wealth creation from business R&D. The budget increase of

DKr 0.4 billion that was announced in the 1995 budget is a good first step in the Government's efforts to attain the formulated R&D target.

Even if so ambitious a target could be met, Denmark is a small country and hence its total research effort is bound to remain small, compared to that of other countries. By no means does this reduce the importance of increasing national R&D effort – on the contrary – but it underlines the importance of maintaining close contacts with international research and of making optimal use of international co-operation. It also involves making clear choices at the national level on priority areas. Denmark has to be selective in order to have at least a few areas in which Danish research can be considered to be in the category "best in the world", and it must also take care to ensure that beneficial results from this investment accrue to the Danish economy.

In relation to the issue of the level of the national R&D effort, we heard concerns that the insufficiency of investment in "basic" research would hamper Denmark's long-term development. It is our impression that those concerns may derive from some confusion about the term "basic research". As commonly agreed by the international community, "basic research" covers both "pure" and "strategic" research. Therefore we do not think, on the basis of statistics provided to us, notably in the Background Report, that the share of "basic" research in the total R&D effort (about 30 per cent) is particularly low in Denmark, as compared to most OECD countries, A second source of confusion seems to derive from an assimilation of "basic research" to "base funding" of research. "Base funding" is that part of government allocations to research which is not earmarked for specific projects and is designed to support "core" infrastructure and personnel. From this perspective, it is true that there was, over the 1980s, a worrying declining trend in the share of "base" funding in government R&D allocations. This trend has fortunately been reversed since the early 1990s. These issues are discussed in greater detail in Chapter IV.

2. The innovation challenge

Industrial innovation is just one of several goals served by research. At the same time, innovation is more than just R&D. As the Background Report points out, R&D expenditure is less than half of innovation costs and most of that expenditure is development rather than research. Moreover, many innovative firms invest very little in R&D; for many of them, excellence of design is the key to success. This is especially true in Denmark, where there are relatively large numbers of small firms. In these smaller firms, the innovation process differs in some important respects from what it is in larger, technology-driven companies. As a result, increasing the knowledge content and quality of Danish products also means providing an educational system that supplies industry with up-to-date knowledge and relevant skills and involves large parts of the work force in lifelong learning as well. It means ensuring that firms can obtain advice on organisational and managerial aspects of innovation and, obviously, that they have access to relevant technological knowledge from public institutes. It means removing obstacles to the creativity and growth of entrepreneurship.

The Danish industrial structure is strongly dependent on small and medium-sized firms. Only about 80 manufacturing enterprises have a work force of more than 500, and there is not a single enterprise whose work force can be counted in multiples of 10 000. This is a source of flexibility but it means also that the country lacks the "industrial locomotives" that could take the lead in technological development through large investments in private R&D. There are, however, some very large firms in the service industries and some conglomerates with manufacturing interests.

One of the characteristics that might hamper improved export performance is that Danish export performance is strongest in sectors with relatively low technology and a low growth profile. The two sectors in which exports are markedly above the OECD average are food and beverages, and wood and wood products (including furniture).[3] This implies that in order to attain growth rates that exceed the rate at which their export markets develop, Danish industries will have either to increase their market shares or shift towards export markets with higher growth rates. The Danish economy should diversify towards R&D intensive sectors while maintaining the high rate of diffusion of, and investment in, new technologies throughout the traditional sectors. The latter has been a key to their good performance, as shown in the recent OECD Economic Survey.

3. The need for a strategic focus

Research and development

The wish to increase the knowledge content and quality of Danish products and the related desire to strengthen Denmark's research and innovation system demand a clear and focused strategy. In many discussions we heard complaints about the lack of a such a strategy at the national level. Guidance was felt to be needed for choosing among projects and allocating funds. It was an issue not only in ministries but also in universities, research institutions, and other high-level research bodies. It was said in some universities that we visited that they had their own strategies and areas of focus but did not know how to link them with those of other research institutions.

Strategy and focus are a must when choices are to be made and alternatives exist. They are especially important if goals are known (*e.g.* "to create x new jobs" or "to increase R&D expenditures to y per cent of GNP") and there are several ways to reach them, but funds or time, or both, are limited. Strategy is also important when structural changes are needed, such as moving from industries with low labour costs and skills to ones that require high skills.

The so-called "strategic programmes" established in areas such as biotechnology, food technology, materials, and the environment have usefully catalysed R&D efforts. But most do not seem to have had the leverage effects that would have been necessary to make a real "quantum jump" (see Chapter III, Box A).

There is a need for a strongly co-ordinated effort and a clearly developed and enunciated R&D strategy at the national level. There has been a political will to maintain a special Ministry of Research with strengthened powers. It should initiate and co-ordinate discussions for establishing such a strategy – of a three-year horizon – with all parties, i.e. other ministries, research councils, the Council for Research Policy, universities, institutes, and representatives from industry and labour unions. Once the plan is approved, including by the Parliament, the Ministry of Research should be held responsible for its implementation in universities, research institutes, and, to the extent possible, private enterprises. The key instruments to be given for such a purpose are discussed in the next chapter (Section 1). Of course, the strategy developed in the area of R&D should be closely derived from a clear vision of Denmark's future technological and industrial development.

Technology, industry and services

The work started by the Council for Development of Trade and Industry on the concept of resource areas (RAs) is an interesting element in the building of a Danish strategy for technological and industrial development. The eight resource areas that have been identified - consumer goods, food production, transport/communication, environment/energy, tourism/leisure, building/housing, pharmaceuticals/health, and services – cover almost all parts of the production system and thereby avoid the ''pick-the-winner'' approach. Working groups have been established under the jurisdiction of the Ministry of Business and Industry for making proposals for regulatory and policy changes in specific domains. The R&D dimension should receive particular attention. To this end, it might be appropriate to establish formal links between the RA exercise and the research councils in charge of various fields.

For each RA, an analysis of the present situation is a good starting point. The industries included should be characterised as to their linkages to other industries, turnover, export figures, number of employees, etc. During our visit, the usefulness of undertaking an analysis to learn which are the most competitive countries in each RA was discussed. It is important to understand where the competition is. The next phase would be to analyse RA potential in the future (five years, ten years), using different scenarios (*e.g.* domestic recession) and taking into account goals set by the Government, such as the number of new jobs. This analysis would help identify gaps (*e.g.* in terms of productivity) that need to be eliminated or reduced. An action list should be drawn up as part of the strategy. If the funding required exceeds what the Government can provide, goals will have to be revised or cheaper ways to eliminate the gaps found.

As in all OECD countries, the importance of service industries and the changing nature of their requirements seem very underestimated. Historically, of course, agriculture and then manufacturing were the key sectors for the Danish economy. Today, however, services account for over 70 per cent of employment, and some are not only becoming capital-intensive, but they are also increasingly concerned with technical change and R&D activities. In particular, information and communication technology (ICT) is transforming the way in which most services are performed, as well as their location, cost structure, and customer base.

Telecommunications and information technology

We found general satisfaction with the telecommunication infrastructure, which is one of the most efficient in Europe; mobile communications are also well advanced. However, we found some rather surprising areas of weakness in a country which has attached great importance to environmental goals for technology policy, devotes considerable resources to environmental objectives, and leads among European countries in energy conservation and efficiency. Recent research programmes on transport and environment, at both the Danish Technical University and the national environmental research institutes, appeared to have taken little or no account of the future of telematic services and of telecommuting. In general, *we found somewhat less attention and achievement in the ICT area*, as compared with biotechnology, although there is some excellent work and the new Micro-electronic Research Centre appears to have made an impressive start with its ambitious programme. Software services and a wide variety of telematic services offer considerable scope for generating employment, a fact which is perhaps not yet fully appreciated in Denmark.

Another area we think deserves further attention is public investment in information technologies. The Bangemann report to the European Council, "Europe and the Global Information Society",[4] recommended that applications for the information superhighway initiative should primarily be entrusted to the private sector and to market forces. However, *existing public funding should be refocused to target the requirements of the information society*. Government has a role to play in applications for a university and research centre network, road traffic management, air traffic control, health care networks, a European public administration network, and municipal information highways. If Denmark was among the first to focus on some or all of these areas, it would gain a competitive advantage and then be able to export its expertise to other member States.

The inclusion of telecommunication and information technology policies in the ambit of the newly established Ministry of Research should offer a golden opportunity for a stronger and focalised effort in these areas.

III.   THE POLICY-MAKING LEVEL

1.   Responsibilities of ministries

On the topic of structure and organisation, the 1993 Research and Technology Report to the *Folketing* concludes: ''At the institutional level there is a great need to create greater conformity between conditions and possibilities to further the goals of increased physical mobility, systematic exchanges of knowledge, etc. It is the task of the public sector authorities to ensure that there is an appropriate framework for research and development work. This is why the OECD has been requested, in the course of 1994, to carry out an international evaluation of the Danish public research structure.''

The public sector authorities primarily concerned with this issue are the ministries responsible for research and development. Since the 1987 OECD Review, the responsibility for research has moved from the Ministry of Education to the Ministry of Research – successor to the Ministry of Research and Technology created in 1993 – which had overall responsibility for co-ordinating the Danish STI system. Following the general elections of September 1994, the Ministry of Research has been maintained; telecommunication and information technology policy have been included in its responsibilities.

There are more than 15 ministries with R&D budgets, and of these, the five major players (Education, Research, Industry, Agriculture, Culture) account for 75 per cent of total public expenditure on R&D. In the former government structure, the Ministry of Research has not been in position to implement, if not produce, a cohesive framework for the direction or co-ordination of STI policy. Its access to the financial, legal, or human resources necessary to do so was severely limited. This statement does not involve any criticism of the efforts made by the Ministry of Research. It is simply that David had been asked to control Goliath without the means to do so. *The examiners detected a widespread feeling among the Danish S&T community, which they share, that there is little point to a separate Ministry of Research, unless the Minister's powers are significantly strengthened and the Ministry receives adequate resources.*

There is no ideal way of placing responsibility for research within the machinery of government, and the solution adopted may need to depend on the personalities available. The problems are two-fold: first, research needs to have good links both with (higher) education and with (high-technology) industry, and, second, there are a number of ministries, each wishing to retain its own research portfolio. We have to say that the solution chosen by the last Government – a Minister of Research with minimal authority – stood little chance of working and, in the event, did not.

The establishment of a new research ministry offers a good opportunity for giving it the means to co-ordinate research efficiently throughout the entire public research network and to improve linkages both with industry and with the education sector. This network includes: the research institutes in the higher education sector, the government research institutes presently under the aegis of other ministries, and the approved technical service institutes.

It is our view that, if the new research ministry is to have an efficient co-ordinating role for the Danish R&D policy, it should be assigned, at a minimum:

- *responsibility for elaborating and making public the Government's National R&D Strategy (see Chapter II, Section 3),* with goals, priority R&D areas, and related actions;
- in the context of the budget discussions, *responsibility to produce an annual framework budget, reflecting the national R&D strategy, for all public sector research, as well as responsibility for monitoring* – in conjunction with the Ministry of Finance – *the implementation of this framework budget,* once it has been adopted by the Government and Parliament;
- *responsibility for, and control of, major national programmes which are supplementary to the core funding of research institutes;*
- *responsibility for periodic external reviews of all government research institutes, as well as research in the higher education sector, and for monitoring the implementation of the results.*

Clearly, the annual framework budget is a key instrument for efficient co-ordination. A more detailed plan and budget should be drawn up for the R&D performed under the aegis of the sectoral ministries for which the new Ministry of Research has explicitly received a supervisory function. The policy for the government research institutes has to be developed in full discussions with their sponsoring ministries. This requires very fine-tuning, taking into consideration the specific situation of each sector with attention to both their research and technical service activities (see Chapter V, Section 2).

The future success of the Ministry of Research in this key co-ordination role will, at the end of the day, depend on the strength, coherence and consensus underlying the national R&D strategy. Co-ordination for its own sake will not work. It must be based on substantive, commonly-agreed orientations and principles.

In addition, the Ministry of Research must have a mission to build better bridges between higher education and industry. There must be clear indications that the Ministry has a strong commitment to industry. As one aspect of this commitment, *the Ministry should establish a division to encourage knowledge transfer and the dissemination of information about research.* This might well require close and active collaboration with the Ministry of Education and the Ministry of Industry in such areas as:

- personnel-embodied technology transfer, such as graduate placement programmes in industry;
- grant schemes to encourage joint higher education/industry research projects;
- publication of information in user-friendly format.

It must be remembered that there are two important paths from the education and research system to industry, especially high-technology industry. The one on which attention is concentrated, because it is perceived as not working as well as it should, is the one which transforms research in universities and other research institutes into profitable industrial products. The second, whose point of departure is primarily the technical high schools, is the process of technology transfer. It is important that the latter should not be damaged by well-meaning attempts to improve the former. The Ministry of Education has made very commendable efforts in this respect for basic technical education, vocational schools and open university.

2.   Advisory councils

The 1987 OECD Examiners' Report expressed surprise at "the large number of committees, councils, boards, steering groups, initiative groups ... responsible for advising, administering and operating funds, grants, programmes, schemes, etc." Their conclusion, with which we agree, was that it was difficult to understand how this system could function efficiently. There are too many bodies, and a number of them have both policy-making and grant-awarding functions. The Ministry of Research needs an expert body to advise it on policy issues, and it also needs one or more expert bodies to decide how best to allocate the available resources between the applicants for research grants. It might appear that the same body can do both jobs, but experience suggests that this is not so. One major reason for this (although not the only one) is that policy-making bodies need high-level industrial representation, but high-level industrialists cannot spare the time for the detailed process of awarding grants.

Of course, any grant-awarding body will also play a role in the policy-making process. But the expertise of a grant-awarding body will be largely confined to the limited range of subjects for which it is responsible, and (for reasons given above) will be stronger on the academic than on the industrial side. The Ministry of Research will also need a policy advisory body which is both expert and can take a broad strategic view. Consequently, we recommend a two-tier institutional structure for the Danish research council system as follows:

- Level I: policy advice to the Government on the setting of goals and priorities for the national R&D policy;
- Level II: administration of grant support and funding of research institutes and sectoral policy advice.

The examiners are aware of the tensions that have arisen between the research councils and the Council for Research Policy. We believe that these can be overcome and that the concept of a Council for Research Policy is a good one. However, the role of the Council should be clarified and its priority functions emphasised. The Council needs to be strengthened to enable it to evaluate properly the strategic plans of the sectoral councils. We recommend an approach whereby the policy council approves the strategic programmes of the sectoral councils according to the criteria of overall national policy goals, while the sectoral councils have responsibility for the selection of projects and for identification of policy issues within their fields of competence.

Level I: Council for Research Policy

The primary function of this Council should be to advise the Minister of Research, the Government and the Parliament on the conformity of the country's current research activities to the present and future needs of the Danish economy, and in this context to identify gaps and opportunities and to point out overlap and duplication.

- *The Council should accordingly be empowered to advise the Government (via the Minister for Research) on the appropriate broad allocation of resources among significant national research sectors and to indicate general priority areas within these sectors.*
- *All research funding bodies should have their strategies and objectives examined by the Council on the basis outlined above.*
- *Advice to the Government in relation to the overall co-ordination of science and technology activities should be the responsibility of the Council for Research Policy and not of the six research councils. However, appropriate mechanisms should be established for the six council chairmen to advise the Council for Research Policy on these and other matters of relevance. This could be arranged through special meetings of the Council with the six chairmen.*

The Council members should be appointed in their personal capacity, on the basis of their knowledge of the research sector, of industry, of public service and particularly of economic development. They should not be selected as representatives of sectors, but a balance among research sectors should be maintained in order to avoid accusations of partiality in the Council's advice to Government. The Ministry of Research should be represented at this Council.

To function effectively, the Council will require the expert assistance of a secretariat capable of providing it rapidly with good position papers and analyses. The secretariat should operate within the Ministry of Research and should include officials from the Ministry of Research together with officials seconded from the Ministry of Industry, and possibly the Danish Employers' Federation or Labour Union.

The Council for Research Policy should submit to the Minister for Research an annual report outlining needs, developments, and achievements in relation, among other things, to:

- *research requirements for national development;*
- *co-ordination and consolidation of research activities among institutions;*
- *strategic sectoral evaluations (results and future plans);*
- *measures to disseminate research and to promote technology transfer;*
- *internationally-noteworthy achievements by Danish researchers.*

The Council would have the authority and the resources to commission special reports on specific subjects from time to time.

Formal procedures should be established to ensure a steady flow of information from the Industry and Trade Development Council to the Council for Research Policy concerning work on R&D in the business sector and the development and exploitation of technological and managerial knowledge. One way to do so would be to establish a small inter-council working group involving one or two members and officials from each side.

Level II: The research councils

The examiners believe that the role of the (funding) research councils should be:
- *to advise the minister responsible for research policy and the Council for Research Policy on developments and issues within their field of competence which, in their view, require a change in policy direction;*
- *to select and fund projects on the basis of excellence, within the budget constraints set by Government on the basis of advice from the Ministry of Research and the Council for Research Policy;*
- *to oversee and evaluate the projects funded by them.*

In addition to the six (horizontal) research councils, there are advisory R&D committees in the different ministries. Earlier efforts to combine the fields of activity covered by the six main research councils with the activities of these advisory committees for R&D in other ministries have not succeeded. In any country this would be unfortunate, but in a small country like Denmark, it should be a source of real concern. The examiners believe that this situation cannot be allowed to continue no matter how vehement the opponents of change may be. The argument for consolidation is self-evident for any economy with limited resources. Denmark cannot afford not to try once again to improve the situation. The first step on the road to progress would be formal clarification of the mandate of each research council, both within the *Forskningsradene* (the research council system) and in relation to the R&D committees established in other ministries. This would be an appropriate function of the strengthened Council for Research Policy which we recommend. If it achieved nothing else in its first year in its new guise, this would be sufficient justification for its mandate.

The research councils operate in much the same way as in other advanced countries with respect to the involvement of industrial representatives. A matter of concern is that the Natural Science research council seems to have too few representatives from industry, and they have not made good use of the ones they have had. Such people are valuable because of the contribution they can make to debate on strategic issues, and there is too much pressure on their time for them to be asked to referee individual grant applications as academic members of the Council do.

In addition to these research councils, the Danish Government has established the National Research Foundation. The examiners agree that what this foundation has done is a desirable part of research policy, and that it has to be implemented by a body which overlooks the whole of research. Hence, its work cannot be divided up among the individual research councils. Moreover the grants provided by the Foundation are significantly larger (amounting in average to DKr 7.5 million) than those from the research councils.

3. Evaluations

As previously mentioned, evaluation has a vital role to play in the adaptation of the Danish research system. We think that *the decision to establish an independent evaluation of a particular subject area will in practice be reached by a consensus between the Ministry of Research, the Council for Research Policy, the relevant research council and possibly other relevant ministries. The formal decision must lie with the Ministry of Research, because it will have to meet the costs of the enquiry; but we would normally expect the initiative to come from the Council for Research Policy – they and the relevant research council will be the bodies best informed about who should serve on the evaluation panel. The Ministry would then have the responsibility to ensure, or enforce, the implementation of recommendations resulting from these evaluations.*

Funding bodies: the need for rationalisation

A recent count by the Ministry of Research has indicated that there are 62 public funding schemes for research, and apparently less than half of these control substantial funds. The number indicates considerable potential for wastage of resources due to overlap and the creation of programmes and projects of sub-optimal scale. In addition, the administration of these programmes absorbs the time of both researchers and fund administrators. Qualification criteria and rules of administration vary, creating a vast and complex administrative web, which it takes time and skill to traverse. In our considered view, Denmark cannot afford this complex structure.

In the limited time available, we were unable to examine this problem in detail. We agree that the minister responsible for research policy should bring about a simplification of the system. One approach, which would be acceptable to the research community, would be to continue the system of evaluations of sectoral research, such as the reviews of agriculture, health, environment, and to include in each review a description of, and a comment upon, the efficacy of the funding mechanisms within the sector.

A database of knowledge obtained from such reviews would indicate clearly the paths to be followed in order to achieve a sensible rationalisation of funding resources. Before giving specific advice on consolidation – which would inevitably affect a number of ministries – it seems preferable to await the support of a virtually incontestable body of data emanating from detailed sectoral reviews. Some of this data is already available, and more will be available shortly.

It seems clear to the examiners that, in a society based on a high level of public knowledge and consensus, it will be politically difficult, if not impossible, to consolidate these activities until the facts and their implications are laid before the people.

Box A

Issues arising from Danish evaluations

Since the 1987 OECD Review, Denmark has commissioned international evaluations of several sectoral research programmes. These include: the International Review of Danish Environmental Research (1989); the International Evaluation of Danish Health Research (1992); an evaluation of Danish agricultural research (1992); a mid-term evaluation of the Food Technology Programme (FØTEK); and a mid-term evaluation of the Informatics Programme (PIFT). There are a number of issues which arise repeatedly in these reviews.

Quality of research
- Difference in the quality of projects, with some outstanding groups and some whose activities should be re-oriented, scaled down, or terminated.
- The importance of identifying and supporting potential research leaders; a ''leadership'' initiative, of the kind implemented by the National Research Foundation, is advocated.

Resource allocation
- Resources are too thinly spread. Research facilities need to be further consolidated, including greater use of joint university/industry facilities.
- Inadequate funding of core activities in some research centres, at least in part because of the increased use of competitive programme funding.

Co-operation issues
- Need to enhance collaboration among universities.
- Overlap in programmes funded by different ministries.
- Lack of involvement of ATSIs and the Dansk Teknologisk Institut, which appear neither as partners nor as customers in the informatics programme.

Contacts with industry
- Need to improve contacts between research projects and industry.
- Industrial interests to be ascertained by including industrial representatives in the planning groups.

Evaluations and structural change

To date, experience with independent evaluations has been very positive and has led to a number of structural changes within sectors. The National Physics Review was initiated in response to perceived decline in a field which had been a source of national pride in the era of H.C. Orsted and Niels Bohr. As a result of the review, the physics institutes at the University of Copenhagen merged into a single Niels Bohr Institute. Prominent scientists now express confidence in the future of internationally-advanced physics in Denmark. National sectoral evaluations, using independent expertise, appear to be an excellent route towards achieving structural adjustment and rationalisation (see Box A summarising the main issues arising from evaluation exercises).

In this respect, we feel it necessary to comment on the recent international evaluation of agricultural R&D. Agriculture and food are key sectors of the Danish economy, and, following the international evaluation of Danish agriculture R&D in the early 1990s, a National Strategy Committee was established; it appears to be developing a coherent long-term strategy on the basis of advice from seven working groups. Within the conventions that govern such documents, the Report of the Committee is somewhat critical of the organisation and balance of agricultural and veterinary research in Denmark. *The Committee's proposals are consistent with our general proposals for strategic co-ordination of Danish R&D and since public sector agricultural R&D accounts for a high proportion of total R&D, we hope that they lead to policy decisions fairly soon. The Ministry of Research should be given the responsibility for examining the implementation of the proposed strategy and re-organisation in a year's time. The same procedure should be followed for the upcoming health research strategy and other sectoral strategies.*

Technology assessment

Technology assessment (TA) has been institutionalised in the Danish Board of Technology. This body has fulfilled an important role by stimulating the exchange of information and participatory evaluation about sensitive technologies, notably biotechnology, and thus facilitating their acceptance by the Danish society. The means and functions of the Board should be maintained. However, there are obvious limitations with central institutions entrusted with the performance of TA, as the experience of all OECD countries shows. *What matters is that TA, which is an essential activity, is performed throughout the economy as a whole and wherever it is needed: factories, laboratories, towns, ministries, etc.* It is along these lines that the Danish Board of Technology should extend its work, in our view, by all appropriate actions: awareness campaigns, provision of guidelines, demonstration operations, etc.

IV. THE UNIVERSITY SECTOR

1. Recent and announced reforms and their benefits

Since the last OECD review, a new University Law has been passed. Moreover, one important reform has been completed, and the Government has announced two others. The reform that has been completed is the one that followed from the physics review; the two that have been announced are the new timetable for degrees (up to and including PhD) and the new policy for determining the teaching component of the grants to individual universities. We shall comment on these reforms, their impacts, and their implications.

Reviews of scientific disciplines

The physics review was an undoubted success, a fact which owes much to the way in which the members of the review team were chosen. Atypically, the internationally-respected universities turned out to have the gravest organisational problems; they took the recommendations of the review to heart, and their physics is now in a much better state than it was a decade ago.

In the light of the review, it seems very doubtful whether Denmark needs (or can afford) as many physics departments as it currently has. Physics no longer has the pre-eminent position among the sciences that it did 50 years ago and, relative to other subjects, student demand is declining in all advanced countries. Nor should it be artificially held up by an oversupply of places; qualifications for engineering departments are virtually the same as those for physics departments, and an average student with an engineering degree will be better able to contribute to wealth creation than one with a physics degree. But closing physics departments, which is what this points to, is probably politically unrealistic. A compromise, which carries some of the same benefits, is to persuade them to become applied physics departments.

There is a strong case for similar reviews in chemistry and in the biological sciences (including non-clinical medicine). The latter area, in particular, has gone through such dramatic changes that disciplinary boundaries valid 20 years ago are certain to be out of date today – and universities are notoriously reluctant to move such boundaries. We do not think that a review of engineering, computer science or clinical medicine on the scale of the physics review is necessary, and we are reluctant to recommend such a review in the humanities or social sciences because of the risk that the upheaval would exceed any likely benefit.

Smaller-scale reviews of research quality will have to be undertaken at regular intervals, at least in those areas where research is expensive, to provide input for decision-making for research funding. We will return to this point below.

The PhD timetable

The new timetable for degrees, if it is successfully implemented, will also be an extremely worthwhile reform. The problem will be almost entirely at the PhD level, because at lower levels the timing of examinations acts as a constraint on students. Denmark is so law-abiding a country that laying down a timetable may be enough to get it implemented; we believe that in any other European Union country simply laying down such a timetable would have no practical effect. At the very least, it will be necessary to monitor performance. Bearing in mind that in many subjects the act of writing a thesis is disjoint from (and far more boring than) doing the underlying research, what should be monitored is the proportion of students who either submit their thesis not more than four years after starting their PhD work, or are employed full-time by the end of those four years (to the extent that they need more time to complete their thesis). It is submission rates, rather than approval rates, which should be monitored; otherwise, universities are under pressure to pass low-quality candidates.

The figures for each university should be separately calculated for the sciences (including technology, mathematics, and medicine) and for the humanities and social sciences, as their completion rates, as defined above, may be very different. If the completion rates are unsatisfactory, there is a very strong presumption that the fault lies with the university, and that its staff are giving research students topics that are far too extensive to be covered in three years. We recommend that in such cases the branch of the university at fault should have its quota of funded research studentships reduced until its completion rates become satisfactory.

The teaching components of the grants to universities, failure and drop-out issues

The Goverment's formula for calculating the teaching components of the grants to individual universities consists in awarding a sum proportional to the number of students who successfully complete their course of study, once allowance has been made for the different costs of different subjects. We understand, however, that the practice was to base funding on the projected number of full-time equivalent (FTE) students, and that the basis is now actual FTE students. This shift seems to have caused some trouble and uncertainty among universities, as regards the actual funding.

The universities may have a strong inducement to lower the pass/fail borderline in their examinations. It cannot be assumed that the presence of external referees will be enough to prevent this happening, as most will be academics from other Danish universities, who will be facing exactly the same pressures in their own institutions. At the very least, we think that *the Ministry should hold detailed discussions with the Conference of Rectors on the implications of this component of their funding methodology.*

There is a real difference between students who fail an examination at some stage of their studies and students who drop out. It could be argued that the number of students who fail an examination could be reduced by better teaching; but we should emphasise that we have heard nothing that casts doubt on the quality of teaching in Danish universities. For a reasonably successful school-leaver, the most natural step after leaving school is to go to university. It is only after entering university that the potential drop-out gradually comes to realise that university study does not meet his or her needs. There is reason to think that the imminent approach of an examination is what triggers dropping out (and if it is going to happen anyway, the sooner it happens the better). *We therefore recommend that every university undergraduate programme contains a substantial examination during or at the end of the first year and that this practice, which seems to be under examination by the Ministry of Education, be maintained.*

High failure and drop-out rates in universities is a problem common to nearly all the countries of the European Union, and none has yet found a satisfactory remedy. The major exception is the United Kingdom, where even the weakest of the new universities only have non-graduation rates of about 15 per cent and where the top universities have non-graduation rates of around 4 per cent. Observers of the system tend to give three explanations for this: *i)* each university selects its own students, whereas in most of the rest of Western Europe anyone who does well enough in his or her exit examination has the right to enter a university – and usually the university of his or her choice; *ii)* there is much less provision for repeating a year than in most other countries; *iii)* even if a student is allowed to repeat a year, the financial penalties are considerable for the student or for his or her parents.

Even if these explanations are correct, it is probably unrealistic to recommend the major changes that would be needed to bring these factors to bear in Denmark. And it could well be that these factors work in the United Kingdom primarily because they always have worked, and that to introduce them suddenly in another country would be ineffective. The most we can say is that policy-makers addressing this problem should not ignore the fact that the United Kingdom does not have such a problem.

It is important to remember that high non-graduation rates primarily represent a failure on the student's rather than on the university's part. Of course, any university could teach better than it does. But the heart of the problem is that university students have for the first time an unconstrained choice between studying and not studying, at an age when the number of fascinating things to do is larger than it has ever been before, or will ever be again. Too many students live for the instant and believe that studies neglected are only studies postponed. We do not know how to change this attitude even in our own countries, let alone in a foreign one.

2. University research and its funding

General remarks

Fifty years ago, a university was an institution equally committed to teaching and to research; universities stood at the pinnacle of the education system and only a small proportion of an age group could aspire to study at them. Now, every advanced country expects that one-third or more of an age group will continue in full-time education beyond the age of 18 and gives high priority to increasing that proportion. All institutions of full-time post-secondary education have pressed for the title of "university", and governments have found it easier to give in to this pressure than to resist it. In itself, this does little harm; the problem is that the newly-promoted universities then claim that all the statements that were true of the much smaller number of universities 50 years ago ought to be true, or made true, today. In particular, they claim:

- that all universities are equal or at least should be given funding and opportunity to become so;
- that all universities should be adequately funded for research as well as for teaching.

Experience in other countries shows that the first of these propositions is a recipe for levelling down rather than levelling up. If a Western European university is to maintain high international status in research, experience suggests that the research component of its basic government grant must be at least equal to the teaching component. No country can afford to fund all its universities on such a basis; and, indeed, in France, Germany, and the United Kingdom the research component of the grant to the universities with less distinguished research can be as little as 20 per cent of the total grant.

In the long run, the redefinition of the term "university" will mean that many countries will have to envisage having universities which are concerned (almost) exclusively with teaching. *In Denmark, at present, we believe that every university has departments which do respectable, even if not outstanding, research; but we do not believe that every department in every university merits being funded for research.* This should not be seen as giving them lower status, but merely as encouraging them to concentrate on the things they do best. Such institutions have always existed in the United States, where they are collectively called "liberal arts colleges" and are much more highly regarded than the weaker universities. In France, too, most of the *grandes écoles* are teaching-dominated, and they certainly rank in public estimation above any university.

As to the second proposition, there is far more respectable (though usually not distinguished) research which academics would like to do than any government can hope to be able to fund. The central problem for government is how to distribute to the best advantage the limited sums available for the support of research. As we have made clear, we believe that the first priority must be to fund those departments that are internationally-distinguished to such an extent as to enable them to remain so.

Government funding

Three basic principles are involved:
  i) that government should preferentially support research that is more likely to lead to *wealth creation* and in particular that can be exploited by native industry;

ii) that support should be given preferentially to those groups *with a good track record in research in the recent past,* because they are the ones most likely to produce valuable results in the future;

iii) that individuals who are rated outstanding by international standards should be given long-term support, whatever their research interests may be.

Discontinuities in funding, which not only cause direct damage but also cause good research groups to spend time in unproductive worrying or in searching for new grants, should also be avoided.

Within the increase in research funding to which the Government is already pledged, it is particularly important to increase the research component of the basic grant to universities. It is this grant that pays the infrastructure, the existence of which is assumed by bodies making grants for specific programmes. In laboratory-based subjects, it is desirable that the basic research grant that a department receives should be at least equal to the sum of its research grants for specific programmes. Otherwise there is serious inflexibility, a major cause of diseconomies.

We particularly commend the establishment of the Danish National Research Foundation and the policy it has chosen to pursue, which is to pick out individuals who merit support; the effect is to implement iii) above. It has completed the single largest part of its job, which is to choose researchers who appear able enough to deserve long-term support. It can and should now be inactive for about five years, at which time it can review the performance of those who have been awarded grants. At that time, it will be able to award some new grants from the resources released either because some of the previous grant-holders no longer appear to merit support or because some of them have retired, emigrated, or died. *Following this pattern, the Foundation will need to come to life every five years.* There needs be little continuity of membership, but we believe that the decisions should be taken by a body not otherwise involved in research funding.

It is for the Government to decide how much it can afford to spend on research in universities, in competition with all the other deserving causes it has to fund. Once this global sum is decided, the next problem is how to divide it up between the various universities in order to get the best value for money. *It cannot be too strongly emphasised that fundamental or strategic research which is not internationally competitive is not good value for money.* (Applied research is quite different. Its purpose is to provide useful answers to questions put by paying customers. Much of the best applied research is never published, and it is difficult to know what "internationally competitive" means in such a context.) *It follows that there need to be regular peer reviews of the quality of fundamental and strategic research in each university, at least in the expensive subjects, which are the laboratory-based ones.* This kind of review is one to which the academic world is well accustomed, and it can be carried out mostly by examining publications, as fundamental or strategic research which is not published is unlikely to be of value. However, the publications must be assessed in terms of quality and not simply of quantity, and this means forming expert panels in each subject. The results can then be used to determine the distribution of basic research funds among universities. *It is our impression that, at the moment, the distribution suffers from too much egalitarianism and too little recognition of excellence.*

Government grants to universities include money for the support of research as well as of teaching. In Denmark, the way in which the basic research component in clinical medicine is provided varies from one university to another. There are good reasons for this, as funding is built into block grants to hospitals which come from various sources, including both central and local governments. *The resulting distribution seems, however, inequitable and it is an anomaly which needs to be looked at.*

Industry funding

University research receives little financing from industry. More generally, according to OECD statistics, the business sector's contribution to R&D in the higher education sector amounts to only 1.6 per cent, being among the lowest of all OECD economies. Other surveys making comparison with Nordic countries confirm that interactions are not well developed.[6] Given the Danish industrial structure, this is not surprising, but it is problematic, particularly in technology-related areas.

In contrast with what we observe in most OECD countries, industry's low contribution to university research does not seem to be of particular concern among those responsible for institutions or among those guiding them in the Ministry of Education. This situation affects the relevance not only of university's research but also of its teaching activities. This should be a source of concern, as it means that projects are more likely to reflect the interests of the university and the research community than the needs of industry, and it may be difficult to transfer the research results into products. *We therefore recommend that long-term industry participation in funding of university be increased, perhaps with a government incentive, such as tax relief for industry contributions.*

V. THE PUBLIC SECTOR

This chapter reviews that part of the Danish STI system, which – although it is to some degree privately financed and managed, or jointly financed by the private and public sectors – originated largely as a result of public policies for the collective infrastructure and remains an area where government finance and responsibility continue to play a major role. One group, the government research institutes (GRIs), is directly supervised by ministries, *e.g.* Agriculture, Environment, Health. Another is the approved technology support institutes (ATSIs); these have increasingly been financed by customer payments for services, but they receive a core grant from the Ministry of Industry and are strongly influenced by public policies.

These groups are discussed in turn in the following sections. We prefer to treat them together since they are all part of the collective infrastructure and are a central concern of public policies for science and technology. This approach differs from that in the Background Report which treats the GRIs under the chapter on public sector R&D (Chapter V) but discusses the ATSI in the chapter on the business enterprise sector (Chapter VI). While it is true that the ATSIs now operate to a considerable degree like private consulting firms and in some cases obtain over 90 per cent of their income from contracts and services for the business world, the way in which these services are provided, the scale of the core grant, the international dimensions of ATSI activities, the interdependence of the institutions with each other and with the rest of the S&T system all mean that the ATSIs remain an essential part of the collective infrastructure and a major concern for public S&T policies.

1. Government research institutes

GRIs developed in most European countries in the 19th and 20th centuries in response to a variety of government needs (defence, environmental regulation, resources, surveying, etc.) and in areas of market failure in the private sector (agriculture and other small-firm industries; generic technologies; very high equipment and instrumentation costs, etc.). Very often these laboratories, although they concentrated on R&D, also provided a variety of services to industry and government, sometimes using their specialised instrument, measurement, and test facilities for these purposes. The borderline between GRIs and ATSIs was thus never very clear, although in Denmark and some other countries, public policies have attempted to demarcate the boundaries more explicitly in recent times.

The tendency to view some institutes as exclusively R&D and others as exclusively STS (scientific and technical services) was reinforced by the general availability of R&D statistics and the general lack of STS statistics. The OECD "Frascati" system for measuring R&D in fact has always insisted on the importance of STS, on the interdependence of R&D with STS, and on measuring both, but in practice attention was concentrated on R&D.

It is of course true that some institutes exclusively carry out R&D, or nearly so, while others mainly provide services, but the Danish STI system clearly shows the importance of taking into account both the GRIs and the ATSIs. For example, the Environmental Research Institute is responsible to the Ministry of Environment, but it produces research results of interest to the entire research community and provides consulting services to other clients as well to as its principal sponsoring ministry.

These considerations are essential to policy debate and to the recommendations we shall make. It would be dangerous to make simplistic reforms that fail to take account of the complexity of the R&D/STS relationship or of the networking among institutes, both nationally and internationally. For example, the suggestion that all GRIs should be removed from their sponsoring ministries and located under the Ministry of Research or some other central agency does not appear to take into account the specific needs of individual ministries and their continuous (yet changing) needs for a variety of special services and research support. Ministries could of course satisfy such requirements through contracts to extramural laboratories and agencies, but it is essential to bear in mind that a minimal research capability is often necessary if the results of outside research – whether performed by government, universities, or industry and in Denmark or elsewhere – are to be assimilated. Furthermore, it is extremely important that all ministries should take a strong interest in research and actively promote it. Their commitment might be lessened by the wholesale transfer of GRIs.

This is not to say that there is no scope for change in the GRI system or the relocation of some activities. It does not mean, for example, that the transfer of responsibility for the National Laboratory at Risø from the Ministry of Energy to the Ministry of Research was a mistake. This laboratory no longer exclusively performed energy research, and its expertise in advanced materials, measurement techniques, transport of pollutants, and several other areas was clearly of broad general value to the STI system and Danish society. In this case, the decision appears to have been a sensible course of action. The reverse might be true for other GRIs.

We believe that a strengthened Ministry of Research (see Chapters II and III) should certainly have a role in relation to GRIs. We think it should be consulted about the budget and the programme of each GRI and that it should play an important role in evaluating these programmes. There is much to be said for greater continuity and less disturbance in the Danish STI system, but this means regular evaluation rather than spasmodic evaluation or none at all. The participation of the central agency (as well as of international actors) is essential to sustaining high quality as well as the necessary continuity within the system. A number of projects, programmes, and institutes have already undergone independent evaluation and, so far as we are able to judge, have emerged with credit. Although we propose an extension of evaluation, it is essential that these procedures are designed to minimise the interruption and disturbance of the work of the institutes (see Section III.3).

2. The approved technical service institutes

The ATSIs have been through some difficult times as a result of the reduction in their core grant, although the increased pressure to look for new sources of funding, in particular from marketed services, may have had some good effects. There has also been a number of mergers, which have more than halved the total number of institutions. This rationalisation of the ATSI structure appears to have resulted in a stronger group of institutes and does not seem to have done any great damage to the range of services provided.

However, *we feel that there is now a serious danger that the level of the core grant has dropped too far and that the future efficiency of the ATSI network may be affected.* Some of the larger institutes are providing valuable services to many thousands of firms. The fact that they also have many international customers and that the largest technically-advanced Danish firms also make some use of their specialised services indicates that they fill an important niche in the STI system and that they have a good reputation for the quality of their services.

Moreover, international experience increasingly shows the crucial importance of high-quality technical services that are widely and easily available to all firms, but especially to small and medium-sized enterprises (SMEs). Autarky is impossible in science and technology: all firms need external sources of advice, information, and technical collaboration. They also need access to specialised testing and measurement services and other advanced equipment and instruments. Small firms also often need advice and assistance on management problems, finance, marketing, and trade, whether directly related to technical change or not.

For all these reasons, technology policies in most OECD Member countries have recently given far greater emphasis to the role of STS institutions. For example, in the United States, the Clinton Administration is establishing and promoting technology advisory centres in almost every state to provide local services for small firms; the French government is developing a network of technical research centres which involve the GRIs and other research institutes in technology advice and transfer services. In smaller countries, where they also play a more important role in access to international sources of technology, the importance of such a network is even greater.

We were impressed, for example, by the level of participation of the Danish FORCE Institute in a variety of international programmes (ESPRIT, BRITE, EURAM, THERMIE, SPRINT, COMETT, RACE, BCR, EUREKA, etc.). Although we did not visit every institute, we understand that all the ATSIs participate in these and other international research activities. We endorse the view, which was often put to us by our Danish hosts, that 99 per cent of new S&T must come from outside Denmark and that access to world S&T is crucial. The FORCE Institute's role in disseminating fairly advanced laser, robotics, and Numerical Control technology to Danish metal-working firms appears a good example.

However, we would also stress that the "1 per cent" of domestically-based science and technology should on no account be underestimated, small though it appears by comparison with the "99 per cent" of R&D located outside Denmark. The 1 per cent is in fact essential to the effective assimilation and application of outside research. Without it there cannot be any advanced technological competence. The Danish GRIs and ATSIs (like those of any other country) need their own R&D activity in order to perform as efficient nodes in the Danish STI system.

This is the source of our concern about the low level of the government grant to the ATSIs. We were pleased to hear that the Ministry of Industry has announced an increase in the 1995 budget and the following years. In some cases, the grant appears to have fallen below 10 per cent of total income, even as low as 7 per cent. Studies of engineering institutes in various parts of the world with functions similar to the ATSIs, including those in the Asian "Tigers", suggest that a level of about 20 per cent is generally regarded as essential, for two reasons. First, the institutes need to sustain an edge in technology so that they are near the world frontier and able to give up-to-date advice to their clients. They cannot do this without some minimal research activities of their own. Second, they need to be able to purchase advanced instruments, machines, and equipment for demonstration and test purposes, expenses which can rarely be covered by consulting services to SMEs. There is a reasonable charge as an overhead on the government grant in order to maintain the efficiency of the STI system as a whole.

Although we were favourably impressed by our (very short) visits to ATSIs and GRIs and our discussions with their leading people, we also had some concerns about the scale and cost of access to the institutes and the routing of enquiries. Many thousands of firms (perhaps as many as 30 000 or 40 000 a year) make use of the technical and advisory services that are available, but an even greater number do not. There may be some problems of cost and of entry to the system, especially for the smallest firms, and we were glad to hear that these problems are now under review. We also welcome the review of problems in routing enquiries through the system. At present, competitive pressures within the Danish STI system between different institutions with overlapping activities mean that a client may not always be directed to the best source of advice. This problem of access, entry, and routing of enquiries through what is in any case a complex system, which does not solely involve the ATSIs, may merit further high-level consideration. A simple "access" fee payable to the original point of entry may be the best solution.

VI.   THE ENTERPRISE SECTOR

Denmark has a relatively large agriculture and fisheries industry. The food industry based in this sector has played a key role in the Danish economy, accounting for about a quarter of Danish industrial exports. Moreover, some sectors of the engineering industry, such as dairy machinery, have a strong position in world trade and have worked closely with the agricultural co-operatives to develop advanced equipment. We have already insisted on the key policy measures needed in the R&D area to strenghten this very important sector (see Chapter III, Section 3). This chapter deals with the secondary (manufacturing) and tertiary (service) sectors of the Danish economy and not with the primary sector.

We shall focus here on three major problem areas: resistance to the growth of firms, which is reinforced by the financial context; increasing R&D and innovation in small-scale industry; and human resource issues related to management and job mobility.

1.   Resistance to growth and the financial context

An apparent lack of incentive to grow in Danish society certainly has much to do with the "small is beautiful" mentality. However, during our visit, it was often mentioned that Danish management and owners do not encourage their firms' growth because they fear they will lose control of the company. This attitude might change if tax regimes that facilitate capital-sharing and further transmission of the enterprises were established so that outsiders can in time be associated in a firm's management and be interested in developing it.

However, it should not be thought that "resistance to growth" is a uniquely Danish phenomenon. Every country has many small firms that have no ambition to grow, especially in agriculture, craft work, consulting and the professions. A relatively new phenomenon is the large number of high-tech science-based firms with very specialised expertise whose growth is limited by the small size of their market niche, even on a world scale. This means that such firms must proliferate if they are to make a serious impact on employment. In any case, the unemployment problem cannot possibly be solved only by high-tech firms, despite the importance of their contribution.

Denmark has a long tradition of autonomous local government, and many compa-nies find local support and activities more attractive than those of central government.

Indeed, relationships with large bureaucracies are generally uneasy, and most small companies, often with already overburdened management, prefer not to deal with central government bureaucracy. In the international arena, the projects of the European Union (EU) seem today to have more to offer to universities than to small private companies, especially in view of the size of EU projects and of Danish companies. This is a situation that militates against growth.

There is also the problem of the availability of finance. Any new company, and especially a high-technology company, has a weak balance sheet; this makes it difficult to obtain loans for investment and growth. Small high-technology companies, especially when they are starting out, have very little collateral, because most of their value is not in capital goods but in know-how. There are, in essence, two solutions: venture capital and government support through soft loans. Denmark does not have a true venture capital market. The sole significant venture capital company is the Danish Development Finance Corporation, but a single such company is clearly insufficient. The political will to create an efficient venture capital market has been lacking. Reducing obstacles to investment in equity financing would help in this matter (as indicated in the recent OECD Economic Survey). Soft loans, awarded on the basis of a solid business plan, are well accepted in Denmark as a means of starting up new companies. In order to avoid unfair competition, restrictions are placed on such loans: the duration of the loan is limited, and the business is audited after a period of three or five years. If a company fails to perform according to the announced business plan, it must reimburse a part (say, 50 per cent) of the loan. We were impressed by the entrepreneurship and technological expertise of the small software and micro-electronics firms we met, but there are too few of them. Moreover, they confirmed the importance of the availability of various forms of financial support during the early stages of growth.

Another impediment to growth is the fact that small companies do not recognise their core competencies and are unaware of their potential to expand their existing product portfolio to new business segments and satisfy a larger customer base. One solution is cross-licencing of technology. A company might wish to use another's technology or product idea along with their own technology but are hesitant to do so because of an existing product offered by the other company. Combining the technologies would serve a new market segment and allow natural growth. *Government might encourage such domestic cross-licensing, for example by tax measures or grants.*

2. Increasing R&D and linking it to the market

In 1991, business enterprise R&D amounted to DKr 8.8 billion, or 59 per cent of total Danish R&D expenditure, and involved 15 200 full-time scientists and researchers. Yet the Danish business sector spends less on R&D than most other OECD countries (0.99 per cent of GDP). As indicated in the Background Report, only five out of the 16 OECD countries discussed spend less. However, especially in small companies, increasing R&D spending should not be a goal in itself. R&D is required when new products and/or more cost-competitive technical solutions must be found.

Companies considering R&D projects must bear in mind a number of issues. First, because the starting point for R&D is knowledge of customers' needs and expectations, companies need to carry out market research and analyse what their competitors are able to provide to meet those needs and expectations before embarking on extensive R&D. At the other end of the process, there is the need to market the results of R&D. One of the problems here is the fact that technical schools and universities generally accord little importance to marketing, with the result that students are not sufficiently made aware of the need to produce products that meet customers' needs. An essentially similar point applies to design, which is in essence a function that links technology with markets and users. *Marketing should be an integral and obligatory part of R&D projects, and major government financing should be contingent on the presentation of an appropriate marketing plan as a part of a request for funding.* Central and local government could help the process by arranging trade fairs and sales promotion campaigns both at home and abroad. In this regard, the Danish Fund for Industrial Growth, established in 1992, encompasses both technology and marketing. During discussions in the Ministry of Industry, we learned that the Fund will be expanding. This sends a positive signal to small companies and should be of considerable help to them.

More generally, the dissemination of research results is a problem in most countries. Good innovations rarely reach the end-user market unless a sales company or person is involved in the project almost from the start. This need is often neglected. Yet universities or public research institutes cannot directly produce and sell products. If research, and especially public research, receives more money, it is important that links are established between those conducting research and business firms so that the results are used to develop and launch new products or processes.

One means of improving these linkages might be to develop stronger industrial networks. Larger companies are often demanding customers and can help small companies understand market needs. Therefore, sub-contracting and networking – as occurs in areas such as mechanical parts manufacturing and industrial design – offer good ways to introduce the concept of customer-driven technology. If Denmark adopts the resource area concept, this should be taken into account as well. There should be an unbroken chain of suppliers to satisfy customers' need. In some cases, this may mean that a weak link will receive more R&D funding than would normally be justified. A good network of sub-contractors can create a strong cluster, with the core competencies and critical mass needed to overcome the problem of single source suppliers.

The science park concept, whereby new high-technology companies are established in close proximity to universities, is well established in many countries, and has given good results. A significant number of new companies have had access to university research results. They have typically started out as sub-contractors to larger corporations and then expanded with their own product portfolio. At the outset, these companies rarely have many employees, and they do not normally recruit service people but tend to do everything themselves. When they start to grow, they generally move out of the science park to their own premises. Science parks thus make it possible for new industries to be created and expand over a period of years. They constitute a long-term investment that requires public funding.

We visited the NOVI science park in Aalborg, which now also has venture capital for new start-up companies in need of risk capital. So far, eight companies have been co-founded using venture capital. Four are still in NOVI, two have failed, and two were sold. This is a small activity, but it is worth continuing. The management of NOVI felt it would be difficult to expand this practice, because of a lack of good management or consultants available to the new companies and enterprises.

We believe that the science park concept is a valuable one, but we have the impression that the number of companies using these services in Denmark is too small. The rules and operation of science parks should be reviewed by an external body to determine whether their activities can be expanded on the basis of existing criteria and rules or whether they should be redefined to allow more start-up firms to join.

3. Human resource issues

The educational system is recognised as one of Denmark's important strengths, and the quality of Danish education is indeed quite high at all educational levels. We heard almost no complaints about the quality of education or about shortages of skilled personnel in specific disciplines. One of the companies we visited explained to us that a comparative strength of Danish companies is the fact that this well-educated workforce is able to operate relatively independently at all levels (''some of our technicians do work that would take an engineer in other countries''). This does not only apply to technical personnel; for example, good trilingual secretaries are also readily available.

A good example of Danish respect for human resources and the importance of training is the largest company in the country, which now employs over 100 000 people *outside* Denmark. This company, which operates in the cleaning industry, endowed its employees from the start with dignity and status, and it now has an extensive training system. It tries to work on the principle of rapid response to users' needs through direct communication with operative and junior management.

An important asset of the educational system is the frequent use of apprenticeships in vocational education, so that young people leaving school have often had some ''real life'' work experience. More generally, this ''dual'' education strengthens contacts between education and industry and helps make the school curricula more relevant to industry.

Two issues, however, deserve some discussion: management and mobility.

Management

It is our understanding that middle management is almost non-existent in Danish companies. This is not necessarily a disadvantage. Today, in fact, many older, hierarchically-organised companies have very high overheads and are suffering from inflexibility; they are under pressure to reduce layers of middle management. However, if Denmark is to take on advantage of its lack of middle management, people have to be prepared to take on broader responsibilities, and they have to have the tools that will allow them to do so. In the new "horizontal" organisation, interpersonal skills and leadership are essential elements, but this should not be a problem for Denmark, with its cultural tradition of associations and councils. What might present a problem is a relatively weak decision-making culture.

Management training also needs to be developed. In many businesses, management is presently undergoing major reorganisation in order to refocus activities on core competencies and on achieving competitive advantage. It is important for Danish businesses to integrate modern management thinking. One way to accomplish this would be to establish, at the local level (counties, etc.), monthly management meetings, organised as informal sessions – rather than as yet another council – at which outside speakers are invited to speak and discuss relevant issues with representatives of local businesses. The ATSI system could also be used to this end if it were divided into two types of institutes, technical and management.

The value of management training and innovation is well illustrated by the cleaning company mentioned above. This company demonstrated that high growth is possible in service industries, and its many effective organisational changes have been responsible for its international success. These include quality measurement, quality benchmarking, business process analysis or engineering, customer workshops, and employee satisfaction analysis.

Another important aspect of management training concerns cost control. Financial control and planning tools often are last on the agenda, especially in new high-technology companies, yet they are easier to manage today thanks to the new and inexpensive PC software packages for finance. *Cost control should be included in company training programmes as a part of training for project management. One way to boost internal training in companies would be to subsidise the direct costs on a 50/50 basis, so that government pays half of the total acceptable costs.* By according funding only to specified topics, it would be possible to focus training on areas considered to be weak.

Job mobility

Most people we talked to thought job mobility was generally low in Denmark. No specific statistics are available, but it seems fair to say that the Danes generally attach more importance to job security rather than job mobility than do workers in other countries, although low mobility is typically a Nordic characteristic. Furthermore, moving from one area to another is very difficult. There are many two-salary families, so that when one salaried member of the household has to move, the other also needs to find a job equivalent to the previous job. Today, that is not easy to do.

Low job mobility also has implications for the overall efficiency and dynamism of the economy. Competitive performance in a knowledge-based economy depends crucially on the ability of the economic system to distribute and apply relevant knowledge. Yet the difficulty of moving from university to industry or *vice versa* which would help to promote technology transfer, also presents difficulties, largely for reasons of salary levels and terms of employment. In a society where everyone is paid on an almost equal basis, employment choices are often made not on the basis of salary or challenges and opportunities but on job security and how "comfortable" the position is. In universities and the like, for instance, financial and time pressures are almost non-existent, and in many cases jobs are protected. *It would be appropriate to strengthen programmes that support scientists and PhDs who take employment in private (small) enterprises.*

An interesting programme at the PhD level is the *Industrial Research Education Programme*, which allows PhD students to carry out their research in industry. The programme *met with unanimous praise from the people we met*. A similar programme, financed by the Nordic Industrial Fund, apparently existed at the broader Nordic level, but has recently been abolished. We suggest that the Danish government look at ways of further strengthening the existing programme.

EPILOGUE

Overall, our recommendations will hardly seem revolutionary given that they come at a time when a new ministerial configuration offers opportunities for making significant changes in the conduct of research and innovation policies. In fact, however, it is our impression that what is most important at present is to introduce greater rigour into the management of these policies.

This rigour should be applied in many areas. A national R&D strategy should be conducted by a ministry that fully exercises its prerogatives in this respect. Advisory bodies for R&D policy should be clearly organised, and care should be taken to clarify the powers of each. Evaluations of programmes and disciplines should be pursued and broadened, and the resulting recommendations should be fully implemented. There should be a certain selectivity in the management of research support. In the administration and financing of universities, tendencies to laxity, which would be detrimental to the quality of both teaching and research, should be resisted. Greater attention should be given to support mechanisms for disseminating technology; they should not be meagre if they are to render a true public service. Finally, the environment for small firms and, in particular the financial environment, should be improved, so that they may increase in number and expand.

Many of the problems that we have raised undoubtedly have their roots in the socio-cultural foundation of Danish society, which is animated, in part, by a desire for consensus and a concern for sharing power and money in an egalitarian way. Without sacrificing these principles, it is necessary to work, with determination and even obstinacy, to remove the weaknesses of the system.

References

1. OECD (1994), *Economic Survey: Denmark,* Paris.
2. OECD (1987), *National Reviews of Science and Technology Policy: Denmark,* Paris.
3. OECD (1994), *Economic Survey: Denmark,* Chapter IV, Paris.
4. Report to the *Folketing,* Copenhagen, 1993.
5. Report to the Council of Ministers of the European Union, Brussels, 1994.
6. OECD (to be published in 1995), *Technology Flows in National Systems of Innovation,* and Nordic Industrial Fund (1991), *Innovation Activities in the Nordic Countries,* Olso, 1991.

Appendix

SUMMARY RECORD OF THE REVIEW MEETING

The review meeting was held in Copenhagen on 31 October 1994. In an initial closed session, the OECD Committee for Scientific and Technological Policy (CSTP) discussed the Report with a Danish delegation led by Mr. Jensen, Minister of Research, Mr. Vig Jensen, Minister of Education, and Mr. Rosted, Permanent Secretary of the Ministry of Business and Industry. The meeting was chaired by Mr. Van Hulst, chairman of the CSTP. A second session, held in the afternoon of the same day, was open to the public at large. It was chaired by Professor Lassen and attended by approximately 320 persons.

Following a summary of introductory statements made by the Danish ministers, Mr. Jensen and Mr. Vig Jensen, and the OECD's Deputy Director for Science, Technology and Industry, Mr. Lundvall, highlights of the discussion will be presented in thematic rather than chronological order. This overview includes remarks made in the open session. The discussion was organised somewhat differently than in earlier review meetings: the examiners did not ask questions to the national delegation; instead, the Danish delegation was asked to question the examiners about the recommendations made in the Report.

Mr. Jensen, Minister of Research, opened the closed session by welcoming the participants and thanking the Examiners and the OECD for having carried out this review. He recalled that the last OECD Review of Danish Science and Technology Policy had taken place in 1987. The Danish government had requested a new review of science, technology and innovation policy a relatively short time after the previous one because they wished to make the science, technology and innovation system even more effective. He emphasized the Government's determination to raise the level of research expenditure to that of the countries to which Danes usually compare themselves. He praised the Report for its clear wording and called it an excellent point of departure for a constructive discussion. He particularly welcomed the recommendation for developing a national research strategy. He stated that such a strategy should emphasize the use of scientific and technological knowledge and enable the Government to choose among research areas. Its choices should take account not only of the role of science and technology in economic growth and job creation, but also of the importance of areas such as the arts and culture. The development of such a national strategy should be considered when revising the budget procedure (*e.g.* in the form of multi-annual programmes).

In introducing the open session, Mr. Jensen announced two follow-up activities to the review process. First, as soon as the final version of the OECD Report is ready, it will be sent to all interested parties for a so-called "hearing procedure". Second, a high-level task force will be formed to advise the Government on the implementation of the recommendations contained in the Examiners' Report, particularly with a view to creating a national research strategy.

On behalf of the OECD Secretariat, **Mr. Lundvall** thanked the Danish authorities for hosting the review meeting and for the excellent organisation of the review process. He pointed out that these reviews have a twofold aim. One is to discuss the organisation and effectiveness of science, technology and innovation policy, and the second is to highlight the increasingly important contribution made to economic development by the knowledge base. After pointing out that the Examiners' Report expresses the views of the review team and does not necessarily reflect the position of the OECD or its Member countries, he drew attention to what he saw as three important points in the Report. The first is the division of responsibilities for science, technology and innovation policies among ministries and the need to ensure their close co-operation. The second is the recommendation of a national research strategy, which in his view would work best if presented in the form of a set of forward-looking ideas. The third point concerns the examiners' view that there is too little selectivity in the financing of public research in Denmark, and he expected that this would raise considerable debate.

Mr. Vig Jensen, Minister of Education, emphasized that substantial reforms have been implemented in the university sector since the 1987 OECD Review. Since some of these reforms were implemented recently, and since their effects can only be judged several years later, this review comes a little too soon for the university sector. He agreed with the Minister of Research's more general ambition to further strengthen Danish research and supported the goal of increasing the level of Danish research to 2 per cent of GDP by the year 2000. He reminded participants that much had already been accomplished in this direction and pointed to the measures announced in the White Paper "Universities in Growth", such as increases in basic funding to universities and greater investment in their infrastructures. As far as priority setting is concerned, Mr. Vig Jensen advocated leaving a great deal of this responsibility with regard to basic research to the institutions. He referred to the crucial role of education in Denmark's knowledge-based economy and, in reaction to suggestions made in the Examiners' Report, made a strong plea for maintaining close links between research and teaching in universities in order to ensure the high quality of teaching and the availability of well-trained candidates. Policymakers should emphasise the research meeting international standards and ensuring reasonably good framework conditions.

* * *

In the discussion that followed, the Report appeared to have been generally well received. Participants thought it provided a good starting point for discussion of the Danish science, technology and innovation system. The clarity with which the analysis and recommendations were presented was generally praised, although not everyone agreed with all the recommendations.

National research strategy

The Examiners' Report recommended that consensus should be built on a clear and workable national research strategy, and this was the point that received the most attention (and support). Although the need for such a strategy was generally recognised, questions were raised about how to organise the development of such a strategy. Several Danish participants asked for more concrete suggestions on how to implement the bottom-up process that would lead to a national research strategy. The examiners indicated that the crucial point was to reach agreement on a clear statement of the purposes of the national research effort. The process would involve both bottom-up and top-down approaches. For example, strategic plans developed by universities, public research institutions, etc., might be gathered and examined. The examiners did not feel qualified to make specific concrete recommendations on the process of consensus building and strategy development. Such a process required different approaches in different countries, and national authorities were in a much better position to judge the best procedures to use.

Several participants underscored the need to distinguish between the different actors in the science, technology, and innovation system (university research, sectoral research, and technological services institutes) when developing a national research strategy. The different types of research organisations play different roles, and the national research strategy should take these differences into account. Concerning sectoral research, **Mr. Jensen** stated that it was his ambition to co-ordinate all sectoral research while he subscribed to the recommendation that the government research institutes should remain under the auspices of the sponsoring ministries. At the same time, he indicated that he would think about ways to enable government research institutes to compete more effectively for strategic grants.

In the discussion, the need for a national research strategy was often linked to the Danish government's goal to spend 2 per cent of GDP on R&D in the year 2000. The examiners emphasized the need to look beyond this 2 per cent goal and advocated including in the national research strategy a "mission statement" providing the justification for the research budget. There was some discussion of whether 2 per cent is sufficiently ambitious. It was mentioned that Sweden and Germany spend a considerably higher percentage of GDP on research; reference was also made to the "Delors White Paper", which has been approved by the European Union (EU) and which states that EU member States should aim to invest 3 per cent of GDP in R&D. The examiners were of the opinion that, for the year 2000, the present goal was sufficiently ambitious and attainable. They felt that a goal of 2.5 per cent, which had been mentioned during earlier visits, was unrealistic.

In the open session, the representative of the Metal Workers' Union drew attention to their proposal for giving priority to ten important areas of technology in Danish research policy, a proposal they had prepared in co-operation with employers in the Danish metal industry. The examiners welcomed this initiative and encouraged the ministers to look at it seriously. They did not feel qualified, however, to confirm that these are really the ten most important areas for Denmark.

Social sciences and humanities

A number of participants criticised the Examiners' Report for its lack of attention to social sciences and humanities. The examiners acknowledged this and gave three main reasons. First, laboratory-based sciences are more resource-intensive. Second, social sciences and humanities are by their nature harder to evaluate (there tends to be less agreement on what is true and/or important than, say, in physics). Third, natural sciences and technology are more directly relevant to wealth creation, which in turn is a necessary condition for research in social sciences and humanities.

Division of responsibilities among ministries

The division of responsibilities for science, technology, and education policy among ministries, as established after the last election, was little discussed. The examiners commended the expansion of the responsibilities of the Ministry of Research to information technology and communications policy. Several participants underscored the importance of close co-operation among the ministries of Business and Industry, Education, and Research, particularly for developing the national research strategy. The examiners specifically suggested using the results of the so-called ''Resource Area'' exercise carried out under the auspices of the Industry and Trade Development Council and the Ministry of Business and Industry.

The Advisory Councils

Suggestions in the Examiners' Report concerning the division of responsibilities in the advisory structure were, in general, favourably received. **Ms. Steiness,** chairwoman of the Council for Research Policy (CRP), supported the idea of a two-tier advisory structure. She emphasized the need for the CRP to focus more on its role as adviser to the Government on overall policy issues in the management of the S&T system. To do that, it is important that it is independent, that its members are appointed in a personal capacity, and that it has adequate resources for carrying out its work. **Mr. Ostergaard,** chairman of the Conference of Research Council Chairmen, indicated that this was a good moment to reconsider the suggestion, put forward by the Conference of Research Council Chairmen, to abolish the Council for Research Policy. He considered the two-tier advisory structure a formula the Conference could work with. One element he had found missing in the Examiners' Report was the importance of co-operation among research councils. Furthermore, he expressed some doubts about the feasibility of closer co-operation on R&D

between research councils and ministerial advisory committees, a recommendation which he had found somewhat bluntly formulated.

Some participants indicated the need to improve the way in which the interests of non-university public research are represented in the advisory structure, for example by having a larger number of representatives from government research institutes as members of the research councils. **Mr. Jensen** indicated that he was sensitive to arguments that the role of sectoral research should be better reflected in the advisory structure, but indicated that he was waiting for recommendations from the task force on this issue.

Selectivity and evaluation

There appeared to be considerable support for the examiners' view that regular evaluation of scientific fields is needed and that the results should play a role in determining the allocation of funds to public research. Some Danish participants had difficulty with the recommendation of greater selectivity in the allocation of research funds. While most agreed that it is good policy to allocate more resources to excellent research groups, a number of participants had considerable reticence about reducing research budgets for less effective groups. **Mr. Jensen** indicated that he regards clear and visible priority setting as one of the main goals for research policy in the years to come. **Mr. Vig Jensen** expressed some concern about the consequences of such a selective approach for weak or new institutions, but the Ministry will, after consulting with the Council for Research Policy, present a proposal for funding basic research that integrates quality in the funding model. He suggested that decisions on research priorities should to a large extent be made by the institutions themselves.

Concerning the way evaluations are carried out, the examiners expressed a preference for evaluations by scientific field rather than by institution, and for evaluations carried out on a regular basis (every few years). In their view, most can be national, although international evaluations should also be carried out at regular intervals. It was also suggested that an effort should be made to involve researchers under 30 in the process, as well as scientists from other fields. Involving young researchers is particularly worthwhile in fields that are affected by rapid scientific and technological change. Asked about the relation between such evaluations and the research councils' task in assessing public research, the examiners replied that evaluations should mainly be used to assess the quality and importance of different research groups within a scientific field, whereas the role of research councils is to weigh the quality and importance of Danish performance in various scientific fields.

The link between research and education

A much debated issue during both sessions was the relation between education and research, especially in universities. A number of Danish participants, notably **Mr. Vig Jensen**, argued that a strong link between teaching and research is necessary in order to maintain high-quality university teaching. The examiners defended the viewpoint that high-quality teaching may be assured even if those who teach are not actively involved in research. In answer to a question from **Mr. Vig Jensen,** the position taken in the Examiners' Report on the relative weight of base funding of research, funding for specific research programmes, and funding for teaching was clarified: in departments that carry out internationally-competitive research, the funding should be more or less evenly distributed among those three components. This is in line with the "¹/₃ principle" in funding basic research that was proposed by the Ministry of Education in the White Paper "Universities in Growth".

The quality of education was also discussed in the context of the output-based system of financing higher education, which was criticised in the Report. Several participants pointed out that this practice had been in place since 1981, but had been changed in 1992 so that funding depended on the actual number of students who passed the examination in that fiscal year rather than on projections. This increased the uncertainty since the level of funding cannot be determined before the end of the fiscal year (in October). The examiners expressed their concern that this method might lead to lowering of standards. They had the impression that there was some lack of communication between the Ministry of Education and the universities in this respect and suggested that the ministry should engage in more detailed discussions on the issue with the universities.

On a related topic, the question was raised whether three years is a sufficiently long period for completing the PhD and whether Danish PhDs are internationally competitive. The examiners stated that they had no reason to assume that Danish PhDs were not internationally competitive. And although three years is not enough to produce a complete researcher, the examiners felt it was a reasonable period for obtaining a PhD. They did warn, however, against trying to pack too much into those three years.

Contribution of science and technology to creation of wealth and employment

In their comments, CSTP members emphasized the importance of good links between public research and the business sector. It was argued that since Denmark has a relatively large share of small and medium-sized enterprises (SMEs), close links between public research and industry were especially important, since SMEs tend to invest relatively little in in-house R&D. Delegates from **Finland, the Netherlands** and **Germany** presented examples from their national experience on ways to improve those links. Some Danish participants argued that, compared to other countries, the links between industry and universities are not at all weak and that the report exaggerated the issue. Concerning the proposal of a tax incentive for companies that finance university research, sources close to the Ministry of Finance indicated that it is unlikely that such an incentive could be introduced in Denmark.

The examiners welcomed the comments from CSTP members and pointed out that relatively little attention had been paid to the relation between science and technology, on the one hand, and economic development and the unemployment problem, on the other, in the closed session. The issue received more attention in the open session because of the presence of people from industrial research fields. The examiners argued that the potential for increasing innovativeness in Danish industry by using scientific and technological knowledge is underutilised. They made a strong plea for greater attention to the application of new technologies as a means of job creation. There seemed to be widespread agreement that it is unrealistic to expect that Denmark can compete in terms of wage levels with the dynamic Asian economies. The competitiveness of Danish industry should therefore be based on innovation and design.

One way to reap the benefits of scientific and technological research in private sector employment is to create small firms in S&T-intensive sectors. The examiners acknowledged that this does happen already in Denmark, but did not think that this form of job creation was used to its full potential. Several aspects of the problem of the insufficient numbers of new technology-based firms, well described by one participant as a problem of combining ideas with money and management, were discussed. It was also pointed out that technological start-up firms need not necessarily have their point of departure in institutions of higher education and that new firms are also set up at lower-technology levels.

On a related point, the examiners stated that the importance of information technology is grossly underestimated in Denmark. They stressed that the introduction of new information technologies will affect society in a wide variety of ways. For example, changes will have to be made in the education system in order to make better use of the possibilities provided by information technologies.

Industry participants in the open session expressed concern over their lack of high-level specialists in rapidly evolving areas, as their own staff is ageing and there is a very low mobility from the university sector. They felt that this is an indication of poor interaction between the university sector and industry.

Adjustments in the report

A few changes were made in the Examiners' Report after the review meeting in order to correct some misunderstandings and factual errors that were pointed out during the discussion. In particular, a section on agricultural research policy (end of Chapter III) was revised on the basis of the affirmation during the meeting by the representative of the Ministry of Agriculture that the Ministry intends to implement the suggestions made by the National Strategy Committee. Other points on which the text has been adjusted and clarified concern the output-based funding system of higher education, the recommendation for a substantial examination at the end of students' first year (apparently already under consideration), and the figures on research contracts with the business sector.

LIST OF PARTICIPANTS

Closed session of the Final Review Meeting
held in Copenhagen on 31 October 1994

Chairman: Dr. Noé van Hulst
Chairman of the Committee for Scientific and Technological Policy, OECD

DANISH DELEGATION

Mr. Frank Jensen
Minister of Research

Dr. Knud Larsen
Permanent Secretary
Ministry of Research

Mr. Mogens Kring
Director, Danish Agency
for Development of Trade and Industry

Mr. Hans Peter Jensen
Chairman
Rectors' Conference

Prof. Lise Hannestad
Vice-Chairman
Danish Council for Research Policy

Prof. Bent Christensen
Chairman
Danish Natural Science Research Council

Prof. John Martinussen
Chairman
Danish Social Science Research Council

Prof. Kirsten Jacobsen
Chairman
Danish Agricultural and Veterinary
Research Council

Mr. Ole Vig Jensen
Minister of Education

Mr. Jørgen Rosted
Permanent Secretary
Ministry of Business and Industry

Mr. Torben Kornbech Rasmussen
Deputy Permanent Secretary
Ministry of Education

Prof. Eva Steiness
Chairman
Danish Council for Research Policy

Prof. Knud Østergaard
Chairman, Danish Technical Council
and Conference of Research Council
Chairmen

Prof. Gert Almind
Chairman
Danish Medical Research Council

Prof. Ib Bondebjerg
Chairman
Danish Research Council for the Humanities

Mr. Poul Skovgaard
Chairman
Industry and Trade Development Council

Mr. Jan Plovsing
Chairman
Assembly of Directors at Government
Research Establishments

Ms. Anne E. Jensen
Chairman
National Advisory Board
of Higher Education

Prof. Henning Sørensen
President
Royal Academy of Science and Letters

Mr. Nils Bernstein
Permanent Secretary
Ministry of Agriculture and Fisheries

OTHER DANISH PARTICIPANTS

Mr. Poul Bache
Ministry of Culture

Mr. Henrik Egede
Ministry of Research

Mr. Henrik Hjortdal
Ministry of Finance

Mr. Anders Munk Jensen
Ministry of Agriculture and Fisheries

Mr. Thorkil Kjems
Ministry of Research

Mr. Martin Korst
Ministry of Research

Mr. Knud Larsen
Ministry of Agriculture and Fisheries

Mr. Ulrik Lassen
Novo Nordisk

Prof. Søren Molin
Danish Academy for Technical Sciences

Mr. Milton Munk Nielsen
Ministry of Environment and Energy

Mr. Christian Ølgaard
Prime Minister's Office

Mr. Ole Olsen
Ministry of Agriculture and Fisheries

Mr. Mikkel B. Rasmussen
Ministry of Business and Industry

Mr. Erik Meiniche Schmidt
National Advisory Board of Higher Education

Mr. Lars Tuesen
Ministry of Foreign Affairs

Mr. Villy Vibholt
Nordic Ministers Council

Mr. Karsten Bergsøe
Ministry of Business and Industry

Mr. Jens Morten Hansen
Ministry of Environment and Energy

Mr. Bjarne Lundager Jensen
Ministry of Research

Mr. Bent Kiemer
Danish Fund of Industrial Growth

Mr. Anders Korsgaard
Research Policy Council

Mr. Anders Kretzschmar
Ministry of Business and Industry

Mr. Peder Olesen Larsen
National Foundation for Basic Research

Mr. Hugo von Linstow
Ministry of Education

Mrs. Bente Nielsen
Ministry of Environment and Energy

Mrs. Jette Søgren Nielsen
Ministry of Research

Mrs. Vibeke Hein Olsen
Ministry of Research

Mr. Bent Rasmussen
Ministry of Health

Mr. Rene Rasmussen
Ministry of Labour

Mr. Ib Terp
Ministry of Research

Mrs. Bodil Mørkøv Ullerup
Ministry of Education

DELEGATES OF THE COMMITTEE FOR SCIENTIFIC
AND TECHNOLOGICAL POLICY

Mrs. B.J. Hoogheid
Netherlands

Ms. Lena Nebsager
France

Dr. Endre Kanlzsay
Hungary

Mr. A. Kuparinen
Finland

Ms. M. Pulkkinen
Finland

Mr. Per M. Koch
Norway

Mr. Torben Friedberg
European Union

Mr. Gérard Links
France

Mr. A. Volhard
Germany

Mr. R. Meier
Belgium

Mr. E-O. Seppälä
Finland

Mr. Berit Mørland
Norway

Mr. Lennart Nordgreen
Sweden

OECD-REVIEW TEAM

Ms. Agnes Aylward
Director
Department of Tourism and Trade
Ireland

Mr. Kaj Linden
Senior Vice-President
Nokia Corporation
Finland

Mr. Jean-Eric Aubert,
Principal Administrator
DSTI, OECD
Co-ordinator of the Review

Prof. Chris Freeman
Em. Professor of Science Policy
Science Policy Research Unit (SPRU)
University of Sussex
United Kingdom

Sir Peter Swinnerton-Dyer
Professor, Department of Pure Mathematics
and Mathematical Studies
University of Cambridge
United Kingdom

OECD SECRETARIAT

Mr. Bengt-Åke Lundvall
Deputy Director for Science,
Technology and Industry
OECD

Mr. Hans Mieras
Consultant, DSTI
OECD

MAIN SALES OUTLETS OF OECD PUBLICATIONS
PRINCIPAUX POINTS DE VENTE DES PUBLICATIONS DE L'OCDE

ARGENTINA – ARGENTINE
Carlos Hirsch S.R.L.
Galería Güemes, Florida 165, 4° Piso
1333 Buenos Aires   Tel. (1) 331.1787 y 331.2391
            Telefax: (1) 331.1787

AUSTRALIA – AUSTRALIE
D.A. Information Services
648 Whitehorse Road, P.O.B 163
Mitcham, Victoria 3132   Tel. (03) 873.4411
            Telefax: (03) 873.5679

AUSTRIA – AUTRICHE
Gerold & Co.
Graben 31
Wien I   Tel. (0222) 533.50.14

BELGIUM – BELGIQUE
Jean De Lannoy
Avenue du Roi 202
B-1060 Bruxelles   Tel. (02) 538.51.69/538.08.41
            Telefax: (02) 538.08.41

CANADA
Renouf Publishing Company Ltd.
1294 Algoma Road
Ottawa, ON K1B 3W8   Tel. (613) 741.4333
            Telefax: (613) 741.5439
Stores:
61 Sparks Street
Ottawa, ON K1P 5R1   Tel. (613) 238.8985
211 Yonge Street
Toronto, ON M5B 1M4   Tel. (416) 363.3171
            Telefax: (416)363.59.63
Les Éditions La Liberté Inc.
3020 Chemin Sainte-Foy
Sainte-Foy, PQ G1X 3V6   Tel. (418) 658.3763
            Telefax: (418) 658.3763

Federal Publications Inc.
165 University Avenue, Suite 701
Toronto, ON M5H 3B8   Tel. (416) 860.1611
            Telefax: (416) 860.1608
Les Publications Fédérales
1185 Université
Montréal, QC H3B 3A7   Tel. (514) 954.1633
            Telefax : (514) 954.1635

CHINA – CHINE
China National Publications Import
Export Corporation (CNPIEC)
16 Gongti E. Road, Chaoyang District
P.O. Box 88 or 50
Beijing 100704 PR   Tel. (01) 506.6688
            Telefax: (01) 506.3101

CZECH REPUBLIC – RÉPUBLIQUE TCHÈQUE
Artia Pegas Press Ltd.
Narodni Trida 25
POB 825
111 21 Praha 1   Tel. 26.65.68
            Telefax: 26.20.81

DENMARK – DANEMARK
Munksgaard Book and Subscription Service
35, Nørre Søgade, P.O. Box 2148
DK-1016 København K   Tel. (33) 12.85.70
            Telefax: (33) 12.93.87

EGYPT – ÉGYPTE
Middle East Observer
41 Sherif Street
Cairo   Tel. 392.6919
            Telefax: 360-6804

FINLAND – FINLANDE
Akateeminen Kirjakauppa
Keskuskatu 1, P.O. Box 128
00100 Helsinki
Subscription Services/Agence d'abonnements :
P.O. Box 23
00371 Helsinki   Tel. (358 0) 12141
            Telefax: (358 0) 121.4450

FRANCE
OECD/OCDE
Mail Orders/Commandes par correspondance:
2, rue André-Pascal
75775 Paris Cedex 16   Tel. (33-1) 45.24.82.00
            Telefax: (33-1) 49.10.42.76
            Telex: 640048 OCDE
Orders via Minitel, France only/
Commandes par Minitel, France exclusivement :
36 15 OCDE

OECD Bookshop/Librairie de l'OCDE :
33, rue Octave-Feuillet
75016 Paris   Tel. (33-1) 45.24.81.67
            (33-1) 45.24.81.81

Documentation Française
29, quai Voltaire
75007 Paris   Tel. 40.15.70.00

Gibert Jeune (Droit-Économie)
6, place Saint-Michel
75006 Paris   Tel. 43.25.91.19

Librairie du Commerce International
10, avenue d'Iéna
75016 Paris   Tel. 40.73.34.60

Librairie Dunod
Université Paris-Dauphine
Place du Maréchal de Lattre de Tassigny
75016 Paris   Tel. (1) 44.05.40.13

Librairie Lavoisier
11, rue Lavoisier
75008 Paris   Tel. 42.65.39.95

Librairie L.G.D.J. - Montchrestien
20, rue Soufflot
75005 Paris   Tel. 46.33.89.85

Librairie des Sciences Politiques
30, rue Saint-Guillaume
75007 Paris   Tel. 45.48.36.02

P.U.F.
49, boulevard Saint-Michel
75005 Paris   Tel. 43.25.83.40

Librairie de l'Université
12a, rue Nazareth
13100 Aix-en-Provence   Tel. (16) 42.26.18.08

Documentation Française
165, rue Garibaldi
69003 Lyon   Tel. (16) 78.63.32.23

Librairie Decitre
29, place Bellecour
69002 Lyon   Tel. (16) 72.40.54.54

GERMANY – ALLEMAGNE
OECD Publications and Information Centre
August-Bebel-Allee 6
D-53175 Bonn   Tel. (0228) 959.120
            Telefax: (0228) 959.12.17

GREECE – GRÈCE
Librairie Kauffmann
Mavrokordatou 9
106 78 Athens   Tel. (01) 32.55.321
            Telefax: (01) 36.33.967

HONG-KONG
Swindon Book Co. Ltd.
13–15 Lock Road
Kowloon, Hong Kong   Tel. 2376.2062
            Telefax: 2376.0685

HUNGARY – HONGRIE
Euro Info Service
Margitsziget, Európa Ház
1138 Budapest   Tel. (1) 111.62.16
            Telefax : (1) 111.60.61

ICELAND – ISLANDE
Mál Mog Menning
Laugavegi 18, Pósthólf 392
121 Reykjavik   Tel. 162.35.23

INDIA – INDE
Oxford Book and Stationery Co.
Scindia House
New Delhi 110001   Tel.(11) 331.5896/5308
            Telefax: (11) 332.5993
17 Park Street
Calcutta 700016   Tel. 240832

INDONESIA – INDONÉSIE
Pdii-Lipi
P.O. Box 4298
Jakarta 12042   Tel. (21) 573.34.67
            Telefax: (21) 573.34.67

IRELAND – IRLANDE
Government Supplies Agency
Publications Section
4/5 Harcourt Road
Dublin 2   Tel. 661.31.11
            Telefax: 478.06.45

ISRAEL
Praedicta
5 Shatner Street
P.O. Box 34030
Jerusalem 91430   Tel. (2) 52.84.90/1/2
            Telefax: (2) 52.84.93
R.O.Y.
P.O. Box 13056
Tel Aviv 61130   Tél. (3) 49.61.08
            Telefax (3) 544.60.39

ITALY – ITALIE
Libreria Commissionaria Sansoni
Via Duca di Calabria 1/1
50125 Firenze   Tel. (055) 64.54.15
            Telefax: (055) 64.12.57
Via Bartolini 29
20155 Milano   Tel. (02) 36.50.83
Editrice e Libreria Herder
Piazza Montecitorio 120
00186 Roma   Tel. 679.46.28
            Telefax: 678.47.51
Libreria Hoepli
Via Hoepli 5
20121 Milano   Tel. (02) 86.54.46
            Telefax: (02) 805.28.86
Libreria Scientifica
Dott. Lucio de Biasio 'Aeiou'
Via Coronelli, 6
20146 Milano   Tel. (02) 48.95.45.52
            Telefax: (02) 48.95.45.48

JAPAN – JAPON
OECD Publications and Information Centre
Landic Akasaka Building
2-3-4 Akasaka, Minato-ku
Tokyo 107   Tel. (81.3) 3586.2016
            Telefax: (81.3) 3584.7929

KOREA – CORÉE
Kyobo Book Centre Co. Ltd.
P.O. Box 1658, Kwang Hwa Moon
Seoul   Tel. 730.78.91
            Telefax: 735.00.30

MALAYSIA – MALAISIE
University of Malaya Bookshop
University of Malaya
P.O. Box 1127, Jalan Pantai Baru
59700 Kuala Lumpur
Malaysia   Tel. 756.5000/756.5425
            Telefax: 756.3246

MEXICO – MEXIQUE
Revistas y Periodicos Internacionales S.A. de C.V.
Florencia 57 - 1004
Mexico, D.F. 06600   Tel. 207.81.00
            Telefax : 208.39.79

NETHERLANDS – PAYS-BAS
SDU Uitgeverij Plantijnstraat
Externe Fondsen
Postbus 20014
2500 EA's-Gravenhage   Tel. (070) 37.89.880
Voor bestellingen: Telefax: (070) 34.75.778

NEW ZEALAND
NOUVELLE-ZÉLANDE
Legislation Services
P.O. Box 12418
Thorndon, Wellington   Tel. (04) 496.5652
Telefax: (04) 496.5698

NORWAY – NORVÈGE
Narvesen Info Center – NIC
Bertrand Narvesens vei 2
P.O. Box 6125 Etterstad
0602 Oslo 6   Tel. (022) 57.33.00
Telefax: (022) 68.19.01

PAKISTAN
Mirza Book Agency
65 Shahrah Quaid-E-Azam
Lahore 54000   Tel. (42) 353.601
Telefax: (42) 231.730

PHILIPPINE – PHILIPPINES
International Book Center
5th Floor, Filipinas Life Bldg.
Ayala Avenue
Metro Manila   Tel. 81.96.76
Telex 23312 RHP PH

PORTUGAL
Livraria Portugal
Rua do Carmo 70-74
Apart. 2681
1200 Lisboa   Tel.: (01) 347.49.82/5
Telefax: (01) 347.02.64

SINGAPORE – SINGAPOUR
Gower Asia Pacific Pte Ltd.
Golden Wheel Building
41, Kallang Pudding Road, No. 04-03
Singapore 1334   Tel. 741.5166
Telefax: 742.9356

SPAIN – ESPAGNE
Mundi-Prensa Libros S.A.
Castelló 37, Apartado 1223
Madrid 28001   Tel. (91) 431.33.99
Telefax: (91) 575.39.98

Libreria Internacional AEDOS
Consejo de Ciento 391
08009 – Barcelona   Tel. (93) 488.30.09
Telefax: (93) 487.76.59
Llibreria de la Generalitat
Palau Moja
Rambla dels Estudis, 118
08002 – Barcelona
(Subscripcions) Tel. (93) 318.80.12
(Publicacions) Tel. (93) 302.67.23
Telefax: (93) 412.18.54

SRI LANKA
Centre for Policy Research
c/o Colombo Agencies Ltd.
No. 300-304, Galle Road
Colombo 3   Tel. (1) 574240, 573551-2
Telefax: (1) 575394, 510711

SWEDEN – SUÈDE
Fritzes Information Center
Box 16356
Regeringsgatan 12
106 47 Stockholm   Tel. (08) 690.90.90
Telefax: (08) 20.50.21
Subscription Agency/Agence d'abonnements :
Wennergren-Williams Info AB
P.O. Box 1305
171 25 Solna   Tel. (08) 705.97.50
Téléfax : (08) 27.00.71

SWITZERLAND – SUISSE
Maditec S.A. (Books and Periodicals - Livres
et périodiques)
Chemin des Palettes 4
Case postale 266
1020 Renens VD 1   Tel. (021) 635.08.65
Telefax: (021) 635.07.80

Librairie Payot S.A.
4, place Pépinet
CP 3212
1002 Lausanne   Tel. (021) 341.33.47
Telefax: (021) 341.33.45

Librairie Unilivres
6, rue de Candolle
1205 Genève   Tel. (022) 320.26.23
Telefax: (022) 329.73.18

Subscription Agency/Agence d'abonnements :
Dynapresse Marketing S.A.
38 avenue Vibert
1227 Carouge   Tel.: (022) 308.07.89
Telefax : (022) 308.07.99

See also – Voir aussi :
OECD Publications and Information Centre
August-Bebel-Allee 6
D-53175 Bonn (Germany)   Tel. (0228) 959.120
Telefax: (0228) 959.12.17

TAIWAN – FORMOSE
Good Faith Worldwide Int'l. Co. Ltd.
9th Floor, No. 118, Sec. 2
Chung Hsiao E. Road
Taipei   Tel. (02) 391.7396/391.7397
Telefax: (02) 394.9176

THAILAND – THAÏLANDE
Suksit Siam Co. Ltd.
113, 115 Fuang Nakhon Rd.
Opp. Wat Rajbopith
Bangkok 10200   Tel. (662) 225.9531/2
Telefax: (662) 222.5188

TURKEY – TURQUIE
Kültür Yayinlari Is-Türk Ltd. Sti.
Atatürk Bulvari No. 191/Kat 13
Kavaklidere/Ankara   Tel. 428.11.40 Ext. 2458
Dolmabahce Cad. No. 29
Besiktas/Istanbul   Tel. 260.71.88
Telex: 43482B

UNITED KINGDOM – ROYAUME-UNI
HMSO
Gen. enquiries   Tel. (071) 873 0011
Postal orders only:
P.O. Box 276, London SW8 5DT
Personal Callers HMSO Bookshop
49 High Holborn, London WC1V 6HB
Telefax: (071) 873 8200
Branches at: Belfast, Birmingham, Bristol, Edin-
burgh, Manchester

UNITED STATES – ÉTATS-UNIS
OECD Publications and Information Centre
2001 L Street N.W., Suite 700
Washington, D.C. 20036-4910 Tel. (202) 785.6323
Telefax: (202) 785.0350

VENEZUELA
Libreria del Este
Avda F. Miranda 52, Aptdo. 60337
Edificio Galipán
Caracas 106   Tel. 951.1705/951.2307/951.1297
Telegram: Libreste Caracas

Subscription to OECD periodicals may also be
placed through main subscription agencies.

Les abonnements aux publications périodiques de
l'OCDE peuvent être souscrits auprès des
principales agences d'abonnement.

Orders and inquiries from countries where Distribu-
tors have not yet been appointed should be sent to:
OECD Publications Service, 2 rue André-Pascal,
75775 Paris Cedex 16, France.

Les commandes provenant de pays où l'OCDE n'a
pas encore désigné de distributeur peuvent être
adressées à : OCDE, Service des Publications,
2, rue André-Pascal, 75775 Paris Cedex 16, France.

1-1995